"A funny and sex-addled, fame-intoxicated look at teen magic. Refreshingly honest! I loved it."
—Will Ferguson, 2012 Giller prizewinner and three-time winner of the Leacock Medal for Humour

"Mark Leiren-Young is one funny guy, as you might expect from a winner of the Stephen Leacock Medal for Humour, and a great writer, to boot. Driven by humour, hormones and the heart, Leiren-Young takes you on a side-splitting coming-of-age journey that lays bare not only the secrets of magic, but the magic secrets of growing up."
—Terry Fallis, Leacock Medal Winner for *The Best Laid Plans*

"Mark Leiren-Young tops his Leacock Award-winning debut, *Never Shoot a Stampede Queen*, with this relentlessly funny and ridiculously honest book. A must read."
—Ian Ferguson, Leacock Medal winner for *Village of the Small Houses*

"Mark Leiren-Young is a natural storyteller, a peer of writers like Stephen Leacock, W.O. Mitchell, Jack Douglas and W.P. Kinsella: quietly hilarious, effortlessly moving and always surprising. Like them, he makes it look easy."
—Spider Robinson, three-time Hugo Award winner, co-author of *Variable Star* with Robert Heinlein

"*Free Magic Secrets Revealed* is a very funny story of the adolescent pursuit of love and self-worth through magic, music, and weird comic books. Leiren-Young's memoir reads like a cross between *Wayne's World* and *The Prestige*—not to mention *Marathon Man*, for the extremely brilliant yet disturbing facial surgery chapter."
—Grant Lawrence, broadcaster and author of *Adventures in Solitude*, winner of the Bill Duthie Booksellers' Choice Award

"There is only one thing worse than amate͟   ͟ ͟h͟a͟t's amateur magic theatre, but Mark Leiren-Young's slei͟   smiling for more."
—Jackson
and h

D1414984

MAY   2013

FREE MAGIC SECRETS REVEALED

A MEMOIR

MARK LEIREN-YOUNG

HARBOUR PUBLISHING

Harbour Publishing Co. Ltd.
P.O. Box 219, Madeira Park, BC, V0N 2H0
www.harbourpublishing.com

Editor—Barbara Pulling
Text design—Mary White
Poster, page 188—recreated by Tav Rayne
Printed and bound in Canada

Harbour Publishing acknowledges financial support from the Government of Canada through the Canada Book Fund and the Canada Council for the Arts, and from the Province of British Columbia through the BC Arts Council and the Book Publishing Tax Credit.

Library and Archives Canada Cataloguing in Publication

Leiren-Young, Mark
    Free magic secrets revealed / Mark Leiren-Young.

ISBN 978-1-55017-607-0

    1. Leiren-Young, Mark. 2. Leiren-Young, Mark—Friends and associates. 3. Magic shows—Anecdotes. 4. Authors, Canadian (English)—20th century—Biography. 5. Canadian wit and humor (English). I. Title.

PS8573.E478Z58 2013   C818'.5409   C2013-900211-1

To Dr. Bob Hogg, David L. Young,
Hall Leiren and Carol Leiren
for all their support behind the scenes
(both on this show and in real life).
To Rayne for her ideas and inspiration.
To "Randy" and "Kyle" for all the magic over the years.
To everyone else who was a part of this adventure ...
whether you want to admit it or not.
And in loving memory of Adele and Ruth,
who always believed in our magic.

Contents

1	La Lunette	9
2	Storming Troy	12
3	The Black Metal Fantasy	18
4	Free Magic Secrets Revealed	26
5	The Naja Haje	30
6	Bud's Good Eats	38
7	The Dove Pan	46
8	Happy Phase	57
9	The Trilogy	63
10	Su Casa	66
11	The Near Assassination of Little Bunny Foo Foo	71
12	Pretty Woman	77
13	Signing in Blood	82
14	Prophet Participation	92
15	Troubled Teens	100
16	The Necoronomicon	104
17	Falling Angel	116
18	The Manifesto	122
19	Driving Age	126
20	Running with the Devil	134

21	General Anesthetic	144
22	Echoes of Confusion	150
23	Little Shawn	159
24	Press Released	167
25	Almond Oil	173
26	Paradise by the Dashboard Lights	183
27	Hell's Gate	190
28	Birthday Presence	198
29	The Gorgon	204
30	Dying Werewolves	211
31	Muppet from Hell	219
32	Raise a Little Hell	224
33	Four Minutes and Nine Seconds	229
34	Bad Publicity	233
35	Manifest Destiny	242
EPILOGUE	Show Biz Legends	245
	Acknowledgements and Escape Acts	251
	About the Author	255

La Lunette

When Lisa saw the blade of the guillotine race toward the back of Randy's neck, she began to scream. It sliced, then stopped ... with a sickening thud. The executioner smiled, satisfied. Lisa started to cry. And her lover's headless body twitched, then lay there motionless until finally it shouted, "Normannnnnnn!"

The arms of the corpse flailed until two not-so-dead fingers connected with the latch holding its head in place. "That hurt."

Lisa stopped sobbing, bent over to look at the man she was mourning and scowled. "Your head's still there."

"No problem," said Randy.

"And you didn't bleed. Weren't you supposed to bleed this time?"

"I didn't bleed? Normannnn!"

Lisa poked at the black cloth where Randy's head was no longer supposed to be and his skull toppled from the lunette—the hole for the condemned's neck—into the guillotine's catch box.

Randy's real head, complete with the long feathered brown hair of a seventies stadium rock star, popped out from the hidden compartment under his fake head.

Lisa turned to Randy, shook her feathered brown *Charlie's Angels*

9

hair, and announced, "Smoke break." Then the seventeen-year-old would-be mourner spun on the heels of her white knee-high boots and walked toward the loading bay stairs at the back of the stage.

"Me too," said Kyle. The executioner stepped out from the shadows to reveal the face of a rugged seventeen-year-old, and shook loose the feathered blond hair of a seventies TV star, looking like a young Duke of Hazzard.

"Hang on," said Randy. "I wanna get this right."

"Maybe we should just use an axe," suggested Kyle. "An axe would work. An axe would be unambiguous."

"Really sorry, man," drawled Norman in the drug-delayed dude rhythms that had made Tommy Chong a millionaire.

Randy called over to the voice in the wings. "Norman, I need some help here."

Norman shuffled toward the guillotine. Norman was nineteen, like Randy, and had shoulder-length blond hair—it wasn't feathered, but it didn't have to be. Norman was a techie, not an actor. He'd done a great job painting his death trap black and silver—from even a few feet away it looked real and dangerous—but up close it looked exactly like what it was ... painted wood and carefully folded tinfoil. "It shoulda worked that time. I mean, the blade fell, right, man?"

Randy reached for his sore neck, rubbed it. "Yeah, it fell. But the head didn't."

"Musta stuck it in too hard. Maybe if we shave the Styrofoam a bit so it won't fit so tight? Did the blood bag pop?"

"Does it look like the blood bag popped?"

Norman was thrown by Randy's tone. Randy lived in a perpetual state of mellow. His mantra was, "Nooooo problemmm," with the no stretched out to include anywhere between five and fifty extras o's and at least a couple of bonus m's at the end of every problem. But as a magician he knew that if the trick wasn't working before opening night of his biggest show ever, he'd look like an idiot. "We already sold two hundred tickets," said Randy. "At least two hundred people are gonna see this. Probably more like four hundred. We're gonna sell out for sure."

"Not if we cancel," said Kyle. "We're not ready."

"I can fix it, man," said Norman. "Just trust me."

Randy picked up his Styrofoam head, leaned over to pop it back in the guillotine and the blood bag exploded, spraying a mix of ketchup and tomato soup all over the stage, the guillotine and Randy's awesomely feathered hair. Randy went as pale as if all the blood was really his.

Norman was mortified.

I thought it was the coolest thing I'd ever seen.

2

Storming Troy

Like all great adventures, this one started with someone trying to get laid. King Menelaus didn't go to Troy for the baklava. Actually, since all of us were teenagers running on high-octane hormones, it started with everyone trying to get laid.

I was seventeen and built to be beaten up. I had long, stringy brown hair that fell somewhere between Beatle and hippie, a stringy build—because I'd sprouted to almost 6'2" and still weighed as much as your average Girl Scout—teeth the orthodontist hadn't tamed yet and wire-framed John Lennon glasses stuck to a nose and eyebrows that would have seemed a little much for Groucho Marx.

On days when my looks weren't enough of a bully magnet, I also had a mouth with a death wish. Instead of responding to bullies like a sane, defenceless geek, I had the suicidal habit of responding to their taunts with my version of a *Mad Magazine* snappy answer to a stupid question, which led to my only useful physical skill. I could run pretty quickly—until I caught a whooping cough-like virus and could barely sprint a few feet without collapsing. Like I said, I was built to be beaten up.

For most of my high school life my dreams were ruled by Sarah

Saperstein. So was my schedule. If she was in a class I wanted to take it. If I wasn't in her class, I knew where her class was so I could accidentally walk by it before it started and after it was over.

I'd been in love with Sarah since I first saw her in the Jewish elementary school my mom banished me to when she split with my father, found religion, and decided to ruin my life by pulling me out of the public school all my friends were in and sending me to a place where all the other kids had studied Hebrew and Torah for four years. Overnight I went from being an A student who'd been given the option of skipping a grade to the dumb new kid who needed daily tutoring.

The idea was that I'd learn all about my heritage, conquer the Hebrew language, meet plenty of other Jewish kids and emerge from school with a deep connection to my religion.

I learned a little about my heritage, Hebrew conquered me, I met plenty of other Jewish kids and decided that if this was what Jewish kids were like I desperately wanted to be Japanese, like my neighbour, Ray Shimizu.

Pretty much the only thing I liked about Talmud Torah was Sarah. I had a crush on Sarah before I even considered liking girls. She was the only student, boy or girl, who didn't seem to be afraid of the teachers—not even Mrs. Grimble, who could sense you chewing gum, and order you to spit it out, even with her back turned. And when I first noticed girls in the way most boys eventually do, Sarah was the first girl I noticed. But I didn't truly fall in love with her until grade seven—the day we took a ferry to Victoria for a field trip to visit the provincial legislature and our boat was stopped midway to Vancouver Island and turned around because of a bomb scare.

This was 1975 and most kids had never heard of a bomb scare. But Jewish kids had—even the ones who didn't go to private schools. This was around the time the Palestinian Liberation Organization was sending colourful envelopes to prominent North American Jews and, if you opened the special PLO packages, they had enough explosive

power to kill you—though mostly they just blew off the lucky recipi-
ent's hands or face. Because my mom's father, my Zayda Ben, owned
a chain of furniture stores that shared his last name, I'd never been allowed to touch the mail. So all the kids on our bus knew about bomb
scares.

As everyone scrambled back to their seats, most of the girls were
crying and most of the boys were too. They were all convinced we
were going to die. Mrs. Grimble was screaming at everyone to calm
down, but sounding more hysterical than reassuring. And as my
twenty classmates sobbed or tried their best not to, Sarah came over,
touched my hand and smiled shyly. It was the first time I'd seen her
nervous. "Everyone's scared," she said.

"Yeah," I said.

She squeezed into the empty seat next to me. "You should do
something."

I should do something?

I'd dreamed about rescuing Sarah from a terrorist attack on our
school, and her being so grateful that she'd actually kiss me. On the
lips and everything. I read a lot of Batman comics, every Sherlock
Holmes adventure and far too many books on Houdini, so I'd memorized every exit to both buildings, including a few semi-secret ones—
but how was I supposed to save the day in a bus on the bottom deck
of a ferry?

The student teacher helping Mrs. Grimble chaperone us started
to cry. The driver looked ready to bolt and abandon ship, in case the
bomb was on our bus since, hey, we were the Jewish school and this
was only three years after the massacre of the Israeli athletes at the
Munich Olympics. Everyone was convinced our ferry was going to
blow up, and what good were lifeboats if the ferry exploded? And how
were we supposed to get upstairs to the lifeboats when we were two
levels below deck? That struck me as the biggest flaw in the "everyone
go back down to your vehicles to await further instructions" plan.

"What can I do?" Sarah looked close to crying too.

"Tell stories," she said. "You're funny, make people laugh. Tell us stories and make us laugh and then it'll all be okay."

Before I could say anything, before I could even think anything, the boy in the seat in front of me turned around. It was Lenny Levitt, who beat me up at least twice a week to keep his fists in shape for hitting kids who could fight back. "Yeah," he said. "Make us laugh." It wasn't a threat, more like a plea.

Everyone—everyone on the bus—must have heard him, because they all went quiet and turned to me. I'd just been drafted as the dance band on the *Titanic*. So I did the only thing I could. I laughed. Then I made fun of the field trip, said we'd never go down with the ship because Mrs. Grimble would get in way too much trouble with the principal and—I don't know what I said, just that it must have been funny, because I remember Sarah's smile. And her laughter. And everyone else's laughter. And I remember a lot of kids—including the ones I wouldn't have minded losing at sea, saying "Thank you" after the bus dropped us safely at our school.

I'd always loved Sarah for that.

And I always will.

Naturally, Sarah thought I was "really sweet." The kiss of death. Or at least the kiss of platonically ever after. So we were "just friends."

Even though Sarah wasn't in my league, I wasn't interested in playing ball with anyone else—unless maybe Stevie Nicks decided she was interested in younger men. While most guys my age were crushing on their favourite Charlie's Angel, I was all about Fleetwood Mac's Gold Dust Woman.

So Sarah and I hung out, as friends. When I got up the courage to ask her out to *Jaws*, the scariest movie ever, she brought her ten-year-old sister. And when the shark chomped that first swimmer, it was ten-year-old Robyn who jumped from her seat, screamed and grabbed my hand.

The first time I touched Sarah was just before I turned seventeen, when we went to Vancouver's annual agricultural fair and carnival—the Pacific National Exhibition—which runs from mid-August until Labour Day, the day before the start of school and, almost every other year, my birthday. So I'd gone to the PNE almost every year for as long as I could remember. Sarah and I went with a group of friends and she and I started our day paired off on the double Ferris wheel. It was a romantic, slow ride that took us up high enough to see the entire city. A very slooooow ride. Sarah looked out at the stunning snowcapped mountains framing a postcard view of Vancouver and said, "Isn't this beautiful?" And there I was—pressed against her—the thigh of my flared Levi's jeans touching the thigh of her flared Levi's jeans. I looked over at her, smiled suavely and ... threw up on her runners.

Did I mention it was a very slow ride?

Maybe Sarah did love me, too, at least a little. Even before saying "Gross," she asked if I was okay. The only reason I was okay was because the Ferris wheel had a locked metal roll bar that made it impossible to jump.

Not long after the Ferris wheel incident, Sarah changed my life again when I saw her outside her locker reading a thin paperback with a bright red cover. I asked what it was and she told me about "Ice Nine" and the end of the world before finishing with, "It's funny. You'll like it." Then she walked off to meet her Neanderthal date du jour.

I only got the book out of the library so I could discuss it with Sarah, but I read it in one night. The next day I went back to the library and took out every other Kurt Vonnegut book they had. Until *Cat's Cradle*, I thought writing was about showing off your vocabulary. The stories I wrote in grade eight had more syllables in each word than this entire paragraph. *Cat's Cradle* was responsible for me becoming a writer. It was also responsible for me losing my A in grade ten English because my teacher declared all my post-Vonnegut writing "too creative." So it goes.

By the time we were in grade twelve, Sarah had graduated to

college boys. And that meant one thing. If I was going to attract her attention I was going to have to do something spectacular—something epic—like write and direct the greatest rock and roll magic show of all time. It would have been easier to storm Troy.

3

The Black Metal Fantasy

Randy Kagna was the textbook teen definition of cool. Randy never had trouble finding girls who would make out with him. A good-looking guy just shy of six feet tall, he had an easy laugh, a perpetual toothy grin, Rick Springfield's hair, an endless supply of locally grown marijuana and a basement apartment in his mom's place with doors that really locked. And thanks to failing grade ten, he was eighteen in grade twelve—which may not have thrilled his parents, but made him pretty much irresistible to sixteen-year-old high school girls.

When he produced *The Black Metal Fantasy* he'd been out of school a year and his charm was working just as well for him in the real world. Randy's motto: "Noooooooooooooo problemmm."

Randy did have one problem though, his Achilles' crush: Lisa Jorgensen. She may have been the only girl on the planet who liked him as "a friend." So even though he was probably getting laid with more frequency, by more girls, than any other guy in Vancouver, at least in our neighbourhood, all he could think about no matter what—or who—he was doing, was Lisa.

So Randy hatched a plan. It was the type of devious, ingenious plan only a mad scientist or a teenager in love could possibly come up with. Maybe it was the dope, or maybe he got the idea from studying *Hamlet* the second time he took English Lit, but since Lisa wanted to be an actress, he'd write a play for her. She'd be the leading lady. He'd be the leading man. The play would be the thing. And, in the play, they'd kiss. They'd never kissed before and Randy was convinced that once his lips touched hers, magic would indeed take place. And that magic would lead to love—or at least sex. Lots of sex.

Lisa looked like she'd been genetically engineered to mate with Randy. The stuff teen dreams were made of circa 1980, she was 5'9" and had the type of open, friendly smile and genuine, contagious laugh that made movie stars millionaires. She and Randy met when Lisa's family moved in across the street back when they were both in elementary school. For Randy it was love at first sight.

Lisa thought Randy was sweet.

Aside from being a good-looking guy with a lot of drugs, an easy smile and a devious master plan, Randy was also a magician. Doug Henning, a goofy kid from Winnipeg with even longer featherier hair than Randy, a bushy moustache, Bugs Bunny's teeth and impossibly colourful tie-dyed T-shirts had just made magic hip for the first time since the word "hip" was invented.

After Houdini died in 1926, magic pretty much went with him. There were still a bunch of guys in cheap tuxedos cutting women in half and making things no one wanted to see in the first place dis-appear, but even the best of them succeeded better as nostalgia than entertainment. When TV was at its corniest and shows like *Ed Sullivan* featured special guests spinning plates or making little mice talk, magic on the tube looked stodgy, slow and tacky.

Henning was the first "rock and roll" magician and through his mix of charm, energy, and all-new takes on classic illusions, he some-how made audiences believe in magic again. Instead of trying to fool people, Henning tried to make them feel a genuine sense of wonder. And it worked.

Randy had fallen almost as hard for Henning as he had for Lisa and just after the first time he saw Henning on TV surrounded by enthusiastic, beautiful and barely clothed assistants, a fourteen-year-old Randy signed up for a beginner's magic course at the Jewish Community Centre.

He learned a few tricks from the teacher, a tuxedoed birthday party magician who performed as "the Amazing Kendini"—who was about as amazing as his stage name suggested. Randy snatched the sponge ball from his master's hand within a few weeks.

That's where Randy and I first met. We didn't talk, though. He was fourteen. I was twelve. It would have broken several natural laws of adolescence for us to even acknowledge each other. Besides, from the first time I saw him palm a coin it was obvious he was really good. And I was ... okay.

Randy might not have been able to focus on school work, but he quickly earned an A+ at manipulating coins, cards, ropes, ribbons and any illusion he could afford to buy from Jacko's—the local "joke shop" that specialized in classy gags like fake vomit, whoopee cushions and pepper-flavoured gum. It's possible the most useful thing Randy picked up from Kendini was Jacko's address. Even though he started with store-bought magic, Randy instantly stood out from other would-be wizards because he ignored the "snappy patter" on the cardboard cards that came in the same plastic bags as the tricks. Randy created his own routines and revamped every trick he bought, or learned, to make it faster, funnier and more exciting—like how Henning might do it if Henning bought tricks from Jacko's. And he started performing everywhere. You couldn't talk to him for five minutes without him making something appear or disappear, or being asked to pick a card from one of the half-dozen decks he always seemed to have in one of his pockets.

But it was the big illusions that really appealed to Randy—the stuff Henning did on TV. Randy didn't want to make coins and cards disappear, he wanted to vanish an elephant. Forget levitating scarves, he wanted to make women fly across the stage—preferably half-naked women. During his spare time—which was whenever he showed up to class—Randy designed illusions in his notebook. Instead of the details of who attacked whom, when and why during which World War, he'd doodle elaborate creations that would let him fly across the stage—if he could only find a few thousand dollars to build them. It was during one of those classes, when everyone else was learning about the Treaty of Versailles, that Randy first envisioned *The Black Metal Fantasy.*

The coolest comic in the world was *Heavy Metal.* It was drawn by crazy French artists who loved battle scenes where people got maimed, bled and died for women who barely wore enough chain mail to cover their *seins.* If Randy could live in a comic book, it would be *Heavy Metal.* So that's where the Metal came from.

"And what could be cooler than black?" he said, when he first shared his vision with Lisa. And who could argue with that?

Fantasy—with a capital F—that's what Randy was all about. He was going to bring a *Heavy Metal* comic to life and put it onstage, complete with a kick-ass rock soundtrack. That was *The Black Metal Fantasy.*

It would have magic, it would have music, it would be a thousand times hipper than Henning and best of all, it would have a climactic love scene where he would make out with Lisa Jorgensen.

After he graduated, Randy started performing at clubs. He also did benefits, and visited hospitals and old folks' homes to cheer up the inmates. He began to develop the show, building the tricks with his friend Norman. While they were making the guillotine, they realized the show could be huge. That's when Norman told Randy about his cousin Jane. "Jane works for Rainbow," Norman told him. Rainbow. No explanation was required. Rainbow had promoted every concert Randy had ever camped in line overnight to buy tickets for. Rainbow presented Fleetwood Mac.

"She's a promoter," said Norman. "She says magic's huge right now. Everyone's looking for the next Henning. I told her it was you."

Randy knew how to make the show huge. He needed Kyle.

Kyle Norris was an actore.

No, that's not a typo—you absolutely need the "e" at the end to get the full effect. He was a serious actore. He took classes outside of school. His teacher probably preferred to be called a "coach." He wanted to be a star. But you couldn't be a star when the only TV series shooting in the city was about chasing lost logs. If you were serious, you had to move to LA.

This was years before every kid in every high school everywhere had headshots and resumés and a self-proclaimed agent promising to score them a shot at appearing on whatever TV series or movie-of-the-week was filming in their town that month.

Kyle looked like the kind of kid I usually walked across the street to avoid. He dressed in the uniform Brando defined as trouble—and timeless cool—back in the fifties: jeans, a tight white T-shirt and a black leather jacket. But Kyle had a brain. He tried not to use it in public—that would have destroyed his image—but he read more sophisticated books on his own time than any of the assigned reading he ignored. And his big brother had turned him on to blues and jazz and types of rock that most teenagers would barely recognize as music.

He also had a girlfriend he'd been with forever—or at least forever in high school years. Kyle was with Wendy, the hottest girl in grade eleven. So maybe he wasn't trying to have sex with anybody besides Wendy, but he always seemed determined to make sure every girl he met was at least considering the option.

Kyle was supposed to be my secret weapon for my grade twelve writing and directing class. He was going to guarantee me an A.

I knew Kyle's secret. I knew he was in love with theatre because I read the newspapers and I'd seen his name in the review of an angsty musical drama about tough New York kids showing their sensitive side—a sort of high school *Chorus Line*. Kyle got rave reviews, but he didn't tell anybody at school about the show until it was over, to make sure nobody he knew saw it. Kyle got rave reviews because he cried—and there was no way he was going to let anyone from our high school see him cry. If they did, he'd have to kill them.

We weren't friends, since hanging out with me publicly would have been social suicide for him—but we'd gotten to know each other in grade eight when I'd traded essays for his best friend Danny's early attempts at shop projects like birdhouses and coat hangers. It was a brilliant deal for both of us. Danny passed English and I avoided the humiliation of failing all my mandatory tech classes.

When I told Kyle I was writing a play with a part for him, he said if he liked the script he'd do it. I acted, too, but I only acted in school plays—and I always had fun—but it was the writing that appealed to me. Since I went to a school with a "progressive" English depart-ment, which meant we had a lot of American draft dodgers teaching whatever they thought was cool, there was a grade twelve course in "playwriting and directing."

Mike Denos, a balding thirty-something draft dodger with a Bay Area California drawl, taught the course like it was a university work-study program. He'd give us our assignments then send us away. Other than making sure we checked in for attendance, all he wanted from us were three original scripts before the end of the year. We also had to direct three scenes and a one-act play. If I could have skipped everything in school and graduated with honours, I'd still have shown up for that class. I was the first and only kid in the history of our high school, possibly any high school ever, who took extra English classes as my "fun" electives.

I didn't want to direct. I just figured if you wrote your own plays you had to. Directors were for Shakespeare and Shaw and Tennessee Williams—or at least for writers who were over seventeen.

Mr. Denos picked one of my scripts to compete in the provincial high school drama showcase. The play was called *Mistaken Identity*. A few years later, when I was accepted into the Creative Writing pro-gram at the University of British Columbia, I discovered that every student writer in history had written at least one story, play or poem entitled *Mistaken Identity*.

My play was about two perfect women who were both smitten with an arrogant, self-obsessed guy with no obviously redeeming features. I've since learned that every straight male playwright has written this script at some point in their lives—often, tragically, in their forties—and I think only Woody Allen has ever made the story work. The only thing I'm proud of about mine is that I got it out of my system at seventeen.

The lead character was supposed to be played by Kyle, who was the type of guy two women would fight over, even without a particularly good explanation. I imaginatively named the lead character "Kyle." But after I finished the play, after Kyle said, "Not bad, I'll do it," he changed his mind. We were about to start rehearsals when Kyle told me he'd been cast in a play outside of school, so he wouldn't have time for mine.

After I lost my lead, Mr. Denos said I could cast any guy in my class, which meant I could choose from three potential leading men: Jackson, a 250-pound rugby monster who took the course in the hopes of an easy pass; Graham, a dope dealer who'd spent the last two semesters in and out of a detention centre and took the class in the hopes of an easy pass; and me. A decade later, I might have made the daring choice to cast a woman and turn it into a hot lesbian triangle. But this was 1980—cable TV didn't exist, and the Internet was barely a gleam in Al Gore's eye, so I'd never heard of lesbians, hot or otherwise. I cast myself.

This created an even bigger problem, because while I felt totally comfortable directing either of the girls to passionately kiss Kyle, directing them to kiss me felt, well, creepy. My two perfect women were twins—my friends Hannah and Heather—and while the idea of making out with either of them was certainly appealing, the idea of telling them when and how to kiss me ... I couldn't do it. So my tale of steamy romance lost all steam when Kyle bailed. The only kiss I left in the script was a peck on the cheek from Heather at the end of the play right after her character told mine, "It's all over."

When we appeared at the drama festival, the adjudicator—a professional actress who looked like the Wicked Witch of the West's baby sister—pronounced my performance "dreadful."

"You don't enunciate," she decreed. "You'll never be an actore," she said, complete with the faux British theatre accent perfected by so many Canadian actors of the era. She praised Hannah and Heather, said the blocking was, "very strong," then dismissed us with a back-handed wave. I couldn't be consoled, not even by Heather's lovely hug.

"She didn't mention the writing," I said. "Not one word about the writing."

It wasn't until that afternoon at the JCC that I'd discovered that instead of making out with Heather and Hannah in *Mistaken Identity*, Kyle had decided to star in *The Black Metal Fantasy*.

4

Free Magic Secrets Revealed

If you don't speak comic book, please bear with me a moment as I introduce you to the inhabitants of Medemptia, the mythical, mystical dimension that was about to take control of my life.

Oryon (alias Randy) was Medemptia's reigning good sorcerer and cosmic protector. Imagine a young Gandalf with feathered hair.

The evil Santar, (aka Kyle), wore a black cape and a gold plastic Viking helmet and ruled a nameless nearby hell dimension.

Gamatria (Lisa, of course) was a supposedly ordinary villager with an important but unspecified *destiny*. The italics are necessary here, and if you'd like to imagine the word being spoken by James Earl Jones—ideally with a lot of reverb—that's even better. But poor Gamatria's destiny was preempted when she was kidnapped by Santar and brought to his demonic dimension to train as his evil disciple ... unless that really was her destiny. Like I said, it was unspecified.

While Lisa's costume might have looked inconspicuous in a post-Madonna world of belly shirts, thong underwear and low-rise jeans, it exposed more skin than any Canadian high school girl had ever publicly shown anywhere but on the beach in 1980. Her shiny black and gold outfit had the kind of cleavage-exposing bondage-wear cut that was normally limited to comic book heroines and haute couture that was much too haute for high school.

Santar also had an evil henchman, Adoma. Adoma wore black robes—like all good evil henchmen—and a goatee courtesy of fake fur and spirit gum. He was never supposed to smile. This was the perpetually giggling, perma-stoned Barry, an old friend of Randy's whose key qualifications for the part were that he was basketball-player tall and he agreed to show up for rehearsals.

Oryon had his own henchman, but since Oryon was a good guy, his henchman was cute and tiny and named "Zephyr." Zephyr was played by a grade eight kid whose voice hadn't changed yet, Marvin Hollander.

It was never clear if anyone else lived in either of these dimensions, or what exactly Oryon and Santar were fighting about beyond the nature of good and evil, but chasing after Lisa Jorgensen in low-cut bondage-wear made at least as much sense as sending an army of flying monkeys after a used pair of shoes.

If Randy had worked out more of the mythology of Medemptia he hadn't told anyone, but it really didn't matter. The story was just an excuse for him to perform every illusion he owned, Jacko's sold, or he and Norman could build. There were escapes, vanishes, transformations and lots of flashy flash pots that Randy and Norman had strategically placed all over the stage. Kyle and Randy were even equipped with fire-shooters—little hand-held gizmos that looked like Spider-Man's original web-shooters, except these things spewed flash paper about a half-dozen feet across the stage before they burst into balls of flame. The shooters cost about ten bucks apiece and the flames they launched were so impressive that years later Andrew Lloyd Webber put pretty much the same trick in *The Phantom of the Opera*, using the Phantom's cane to shoot the flames. That ten-buck trick scored the biggest oohs and ahs of the show outside of the falling chandelier.

Kyle and Randy loved practising with the fireshooters. Norman loved setting off flash pots. Lisa loved going outside to smoke.

In the script, Santar was always wearing a helmet. This was in the midst of *Star Wars* mania—and that meant every proper villain wore a helmet like Darth Vader. But Randy hadn't modelled Santar after Vader—the inspiration was the original man in the iron mask ... Dr. Victor von Doom, arch-nemesis of Reed Richards and the Fantastic Four, and the hereditary king of Latveria.

Kyle had read Randy's script and loved the idea of playing the villain. He loved the idea of learning magic. And he loved the idea of acting in a show for a real audience—and getting a cut of the ticket sales. But he wasn't remotely keen on wearing a plastic helmet. "I can't see through it," he announced at the first rehearsal. So Norman carved the plastic again and made wider eyeholes.

"It's not comfortable," said Kyle. "What if I only wear it for battle?" Kyle suggested.

"But your face is supposed to be mutilated," said Randy.

"If I wear makeup under this it'll smear all over the place when I take off the helmet," said Kyle. "Maybe if we had a designer helmet ..."

"It'd cost like," Norman pulled a number out of thin air, "a hundred bucks to do a designer helmet."

"We can't afford a hundred dollars," said Randy.

So Randy agreed that Kyle would just wear the helmet for battles.

Then, during a rehearsal, Kyle pulled off the helmet after a battle scene and Lisa, Randy, Norman and especially Barry laughed. Kyle had a terminal case of helmet head. Kyle was not amused. "I'm an actor," he said, as if this explained everything. "I'm not wearing this." Kyle eventually calmed himself and his hair down and everyone stopped laughing—except Barry.

Kyle wasn't amused. "Barry!"

"We have to do it again," said Randy.

"Sorry," said Barry. And he went back to laughing.

Kyle tossed his helmet off the stage. "I can't do this." Then Kyle followed the helmet and Randy followed Kyle. As Randy chased Kyle offstage, Barry's laughter grew into snorts.

"He's stoned," said Kyle.

"He'll be fine."

"He'll laugh during the show. I thought you wanted to do something professional. If you don't want this to be good ..."

Randy couldn't believe it. Was Kyle threatening to quit? It sounded like he was threatening to quit. "It's gonna be good."

Kyle looked back at the stage. Barry was doubled over now. Howling. "Not with him."

That's when the laughter stopped and they realized Barry had been sort of, almost, kind of listening. "This is bullshit," said Barry. Then he yanked off a clump of his fake beard. "Total bullshit."

"You've got to wear it," said Randy.

"I don't got to do anything."

Randy only hesitated a moment. "You do if you want to be in the show."

Barry couldn't believe it. He didn't care, but he still couldn't believe it. "You firing me?" Before Randy could respond, Barry started laughing again.

And even though he'd never seen her, the image of Norman's cousin Jane the promoter flashed before Randy's eyes as he answered, "Yeah."

"Cool," said Barry. He started laughing again as he shuffled out the back door and changed my life.

5

The Naja Haje

hated the JCC. It was where I discovered I couldn't swim—at least not without glasses. And since I wasn't allowed to wear glasses in the water, I couldn't swim. It was where I joined the Cub Scouts and was forced to wear khaki shorts and a green Cub Scout cap that made me look like a lost Christmas elf. My only memory of Scouts, before I went home vowing I'd never go back, was running away from Lenny Levitt, who had caught me, punched me and stolen my only merit badge. I think my badge was for something seriously macho like ... comic collecting.

Then there was a very non-Jewish Halloween festival where my younger brother, David, and I were blindfolded and led through a section of the varnish-scented auditorium where people howled and moaned and we had to stick our hands into bowls of cold pasta and peeled grapes that some older kid told us were entrails and eyeballs. David was scared. I might have been too—but I was pretty sure no one was going to let high school kids get their hands on entrails and eyeballs.

So I'd never been fond of the JCC—or the auditorium—which was a shame since it was only a dozen doors down the alley from my house. But Sarah was taking a Hebrew class after school at the JCC and since she knew I lived nearby we walked there together. She went to her class and I walked by the auditorium to get to the exit closest to home. That's when I heard Randy shout, "The blood bag didn't break. Again."

"Sorry, man," said Norman.

"This is a joke," said Kyle. "We don't even have an Adoma anymore and we open in a week."

And that's when I poked my head in the auditorium door and saw Lisa in her demon-spawn harem outfit. Princess Leia was still a few months away from appearing on screen in her chain-mail bikini. The most risqué thing anyone had ever seen in pop culture was a photo of Farrah Fawcett in a one-piece red bathing suit where you could see how cold it was when the photo was taken. This was definitely a more innocent age. "Hey," I said.

Lisa nodded in my direction and kept walking.

"Hey," said Kyle.

"Mark, right?" asked Randy.

"Yeah," I said.

"Yeah," said Randy. "We're doing a show."

"Maybe," said Kyle.

Randy flinched, then recovered. "We're doing a magic show."

"I don't remember Kendini teaching us about guillotines."

Randy laughed. "I forgot you were in that class."

I hadn't realized he'd known I was in that class.

"You invented that matchbox trick."

I couldn't believe he remembered.

Sarah Saperstein wasn't my only crush. Like Randy, I was also crazy about Henning. Just the idea that someone from Canada could be the best in the world at anything was exciting. I was also smitten with a TV show starring Bill Bixby as a magician who used his skills to solve crimes. And when I was a little kid my Grandpa Chase used to pull coins from my ear and do card tricks that I always thought

31

were, well, magic. I was one of those kids who always looked at the ads on the back of the comic books: "Free Magic Secrets Revealed— Astonish your friends and impress the girls!" But I was more interested in understanding tricks than performing them.

Kendini had shown us a plastic "vanishing box" that made coins disappear, but even if you couldn't see the trap doors, the thing looked like it was gimmicked. It was hard to imagine anyone over the age of six not realizing that nothing remotely magical had happened. I looked at it, saw how the false panel on the bottom worked, went home and experimented with creating a similar false bottom in an ordinary sliding matchbox. When I performed my trick for the class, everyone was impressed but Kendini. He'd seemed kind of pissed off, grabbed the matchbox from me and, before I could object, started taking it apart in front of the class. After he discovered the false bottom and the missing penny, he rendered his verdict. "Clever," he said. Then he handed me back my now-mangled homemade trick. As soon as the class was over I tossed it in the garbage.

I was especially fascinated by where magic came from. I wasn't particularly interested in how tricks were done, so much as what kinds of things were possible. Instead of studying Kendini's mimeographed diagrams and corny patter, I'd gone to the library and taken out books on Houdini and his inspiration, the great French magician Robert Houdin. Then my mom bought me a book that became my instant favourite—a history of ancient magic. So while I was supposed to be memorizing the routine for "cups and balls," I was obsessing over everything from the tricks that convinced people the Delphic temples were run by mystic oracles to the kind of snake magic historians believe Moses used when he transformed a stick into a serpent and scared the hell out of the pharaoh. According to my bible, Walter B. Gibson's *Secrets of Magic*, it was an Egyptian cobra, the *naja haje*—a nasty asp that can be temporarily paralyzed if you apply the right pressure just below its head.

When a sorcerer—or saviour—threw the *naja haje* to the ground, the angry snake would snap out of its trance and start doing the slithering snake thing. The trick was obviously a big hit at Egyptian birthday parties, weddings and bar mitzvahs.

For my one and only birthday party appearance as a magician, I hooked up with another kid from Kendini's class, my friend Ari. I wrote our patter and came up with the routine, but Ari did most of the performing, partly because he owned more tricks than I did. My cousin Adam and his two dozen seven-year-old friends were impressed enough to shut up and watch us take over their living room for about fifteen minutes. They were especially enthusiastic after we used Ari's "magic pan" to turn a few broken eggs and a mess of ingredients into chocolate cupcakes—so my auntie Judy paid us twenty bucks. Even though the show was a success, I'd decided to retire after that. I never needed to perform magic again ... but I still loved watching it.

"What kind of show are you doing?" I asked.

"It's a rock and roll magic show," said Randy.

"It's a play," said Kyle. "Two sorcerors fighting over their disciple."

"Cool," I said. It was pretty obvious the disciple was Lisa.

"We've already sold three hundred tickets," said Randy.

I didn't know what to say to that. I was incredulous, impressed, jealous. It was pretty obvious why Kyle chose this over my play.

"Wanna buy a ticket?" said Randy. "Only a buck fifty for students."

Before I could answer, I saw the look on Kyle's face. It was almost possible to hear the tumblers clicking into place. "You act," said Kyle.

"Sometimes."

"And you're tall?" said Kyle.

He phrased it like a question, so I said, "Yeah"—but now I was getting nervous.

"And you were in Kendini's class," said Randy. "You know magic."

"Well, I haven't practised since we were kids, except for some escapes but ..."

Randy and Kyle exchanged smiles, then Randy grinned like a game show host. "Wanna be a star?"

Before I could answer, Kyle chimed in again. "He'll look great with the beard."

"Get up here," said Randy. "You've got lines to learn."

It never crossed my mind to do anything besides what I did next—jump onstage. I only had one question. I asked Kyle when Randy went outside to get Lisa. What did a magic show about a demon dimension have to do with the Jewish Community Centre?

"Randy's dad works here. As long as no one else has it booked we get the place for free."

By the time Lisa was back from her smoke break I had Barry's goatee glued to my chin.

I soon discovered that I had to wear a helmet, too. And so did the grade eight kid, Marvin.

Although everyone remembers Houdini for his underwater escapes and handcuff challenges, the trick that first made him famous was "The Metamorphosis," which was his classic escape. It's pretty much *the* classic escape—and the prototype for almost everything every magician has miraculously escaped from ever since. Houdini was chained, stuffed into a sack and thrown into a crate. His assistant—originally his wife, Beth, would stand over the crate, lift a curtain and one, two, three ...

When the curtain fell Houdini was there, posing triumphantly on the box.

Magic.

Then Houdini would undo all the locks and open the crate to reveal that Beth was inside, now wearing the same shackles the master escape artist had miraculously shed.

Randy couldn't afford to buy the box—it would have cost thousands of dollars from a big US magic shop—and he wasn't sure he could build one, but he'd figured out a way to perform his own Metamorphosis. Instead of a crate he'd use a helmet. Oryon would summon another powerful good wizard, or demigod, or spirit, or benevolent all-powerful mystic creature to help in the battle against

Santar and, in order to conjure this ally, he would need Zephyr's help. Marvin/Zephyr would put on a helmet that covered his head and Randy/Oryon would circle around him, holding his mother's purple silk bedsheet. Zephyr would take one end of the sheet. The other would be held by Oryon until it was passed to Norman—who had no secret identity and was holding it offstage. As soon as Norman had his end of the bedsheet, Adoma (that would be me) crawled as quickly as possible onstage and slipped under the helmet Zephyr was holding. Then Zephyr crawled offstage—hidden by the sheet—and Randy wrapped the sheet around me, although the audience assumed he was wrapping Zephyr/Marvin.

Magicians aren't supposed to share their secrets, even under threat of death, so I wouldn't normally reveal the tricks to a magic trick, but I doubt there are a lot of magicians building their careers around an illusion that requires their mom's bedsheet.

After I was in place, Oryon would do his mystic summoning ritual and Zephyr would slowly, ever so slowly, begin to grow. Marvin was a shade over 4'. I was almost 6'2". That's why Kyle was so excited about my height. While Oryon was still gawking at his minion's transformation, I'd start to laugh—a maniacal evil villain cackle—then throw off my helmet to reveal …

"Adoma!" Oryon would shout. "How did you breach my mystical defences? What have you done to Zephyr?"

It sounded cheesy and obvious and when I rehearsed it, it felt cheesy and obvious. I definitely got how this would have cracked Barry up. It made me want to laugh, too, and I wasn't stoned. But by dress rehearsal, Marvin and I managed to get the switch down to a few seconds. Even Kyle was impressed. Randy had figured out how to do the Metamorphosis—a legendary transformation—with a borrowed bedsheet and a toy helmet he'd liberated from the JCC daycare.

Once I appeared, I delivered my message from Santar in quasi-olde English telling Oryon he was doomed and would never rescue Gamatria. Then, as I screamed, "Prepare to d …" Oryon would zap me with a mystic whammy and I'd wander offstage like a zombie. Very cool. After Zephyr and I conquered our transformation, it was time for Randy to rehearse the big finale.

Oryon was finally, finally, leaning over to kiss Gamatria when Lisa pulled away. "Why do I have to kiss you?"

"Because it's in the script. Oryon just rescued you and ..." Randy looked like he was drowning.

"I know it's in the script," said Lisa, "but it doesn't make sense. I mean, she's Santar's disciple, right? He's been brainwashing her for, like, years. So why would she suddenly be all over Oryon? Wouldn't she think he was the villain?"

"But she was supposed to be Oryon's disciple and Santar kidnapped her and ..." Randy pleaded, almost whined, "they're soulmates."

Lisa wasn't sold. "I think she'd be afraid of him. Mark, you're a writer. Do you think it makes sense?"

It was the first time Lisa had really spoken to me. And she wasn't just acknowledging me, she knew I was a writer. We'd been in a few classes together, but I didn't think she'd ever noticed me. My zombie trance shattered. I looked over at her and tried to focus on her eyes and not her low-cut top.

"Well, Oryon does rescue her," I said.

"Exactly," said Randy. "See, Oryon rescues her."

"But Gamatria still wouldn't trust him," I continued. "It might be more powerful if Oryon is desperately in love with her but ..." I grinned, I really liked this next idea. "She doesn't remember him. Like a mystic amnesia spell."

"That's cool," said Lisa. "I like that."

"Me too," said Kyle. "It's way more powerful."

I couldn't believe the girl in the harem outfit was excited about my ideas. "You know what might be really cool? If Gamatria made out with Santar and Oryon had to watch—so you'd see his heart breaking. Then he'd really want to kill Santar."

"I like that," said Lisa. "That's nasty."

"Yeah," said Kyle. "That has layers to it."

"No," said Randy with surprising intensity. "It's too late to make changes."

"Well, I'm not kissing Oryon," she said. "It doesn't make sense."

"Let's just try it once," suggested Randy. "I mean, Oryon is rescuing you."

"But she thinks he's kidnapping her," I said. "Wouldn't she try to kill him?"

If Randy had any real magic powers he would have made the rest of us disappear while he rehearsed his big love scene with Lisa.

Instead, Norman interrupted. "We've got to get back to it. They're kicking us out at ten."

"No kiss," said Lisa.

"You're right," said Randy softly. "It doesn't make sense."

None of us understood why Randy never quite looked happy that week—even after we sold out all four hundred tickets.

6

Bud's Good Eats

Randy and Norman double-checked the props, triple-checked the flash pots, and quadruple-checked the guillotine. If a head didn't roll at showtime, heads were definitely going to roll afterwards. But that wasn't the biggest thing Randy was worrying about. "Is she here?"

Norman nodded. "She's coming, man."

"That's good," said Randy. "That's good."

Randy had never been nervous about a show before. And even though this was his baby—he wrote the script, directed it and starred as Oryon—only one thing scared him. Cousin Jane.

I was scared, too, because I'd given Sarah two tickets. She was bringing her younger sister, Robyn, which wasn't a thrill, but at least she didn't invite a date. And she seemed to be into older guys—maybe she'd like the fake beard.

Kyle was scared because it was the biggest audience he'd ever performed for. And he wasn't expecting the guillotine—or the show—to work.

Lisa was scared because her parents were showing up and she wasn't sure how they would react to her costume. I was pretty sure they wouldn't like it nearly as much as we did.

We got into our costumes, smeared on our makeup and Norman hit the preshow music, which kicked off with *The Grand Illusion* by Styx.

Our illusions may not have been grand, but for $2.50 a ticket for adults and $1.50 for students, they were damn good. The flash pots flashed. The fire-shooters fired. When it was time for the Metamorphosis, Marvin and I metamorphosized. The effect might not have rivalled Houdini's, but it scored the same shocked gasps that make magic shows magical for audiences and performers. The audience was still oohing at Zephyr's miraculous growth spurt when the helmet flew off and they realized he'd been transformed into Adoma. Me. Some people screamed. As I stood there in my trance, I saw Sarah in the third row and had to force myself not to smile.

Then Santar captured Oryon and I strapped him into the guillotine while Pink Floyd's *Careful with That Axe, Eugene* blasted out of the auditorium's tinny speakers. As the audience held their breath, so did everyone onstage. Randy's Styrofoam head fell straight into the bucket and blood sprayed everywhere. The audience screamed again.

Kyle didn't wear his helmet and Santar's hair looked perfect.

We didn't get a standing ovation, but we managed two curtain calls and some of the little kids stuck around to get Randy, Kyle and Lisa to sign their programs.

Marvin went straight home with his parents. Kyle's girlfriend, Wendy, kissed him and then took off. Lisa's parents complimented her on the show and didn't even mention her costume—at least not until she got home. I went into the auditorium to find Sarah, but she wasn't there. So I retreated backstage to take off my beard.

By the time I had cleaned up, changed and wandered back onstage, no one was in the auditorium except the cast, and everyone but Randy had changed back into their jeans and T-shirts. Randy was still in his white wizard robes when Norman opened the auditorium door and walked in with a woman so stunning she made Lisa look like Marvin. Lisa was gorgeous, but Lisa was seventeen and gorgeous.

Cousin Jane was twenty-two and built like a *Playboy* centrefold minus the staples.

"I'm Jane," said cousin Jane.

"Me Tarzan," said Randy.

"You're cute," she said.

"I'm Kyle," said Kyle, trying to look cuter than Randy.

"You were great," said Jane. Then she took Kyle's hand and he looked like he was going to melt.

"You too," said Jane, as she flashed a smile at Randy. "Nice work."

Then, while both of them stammered out thank yous, Jane looked at me—or maybe through me. "Norman says you're a writer," said Jane. "He says you're really good." I'd forgotten Norman was in my creative writing class. Now it was my turn to stammer. "I liked the beard," she said. "Sexy."

"Jane works with Rainbow," said Randy.

Just as this was registering for me and Kyle and Lisa, Jane added, "I work with their new theatre division. I'm handling the *Beatlemania* tour."

Beatlemania? The show was touring everywhere. It was a cross between a tribute band and a stage play and it was selling out around the world. None of us had seen it because none of us was old enough to remember Paul McCartney before he started Wings, but we all knew it was huge. "We've only done two stage shows in our history—*Beatlemania* and *A Chorus Line*. I think you should be our third."

Kyle laughed. "So you think we're the next *Beatlemania*?"

Jane didn't laugh, didn't even smile, just looked at us like we were money. "I think you've got something here, something fresh." She gestured to the stage that was still drenched in fake blood. "I think this could be big."

Big? Someone from Rainbow thought we could be big?

"Wanna go for a drink?" Jane asked.

Drinking age in BC was nineteen.

Randy and Norman were nineteen. Lisa looked nineteen. Kyle had a fake ID. Even though I was a few months away from eighteen I wasn't going to be fooling anyone. So when we went to celebrate at Bud's Good Eats, a converted garage-turned-cowboy-diner that served Tex-Mex nachos and cheap beer, I was about to order a Coke when Jane told the waiter she was buying and ordered a round of Coronas for her friends.

The waiter, who looked like a heftier, unhealthier version of John Belushi in his *Saturday Night Live* cheeseburger sketch, glared at me and started to say something when Jane flashed her playmate smile. Belushi responded with what looked like an attempt at a grin, surrendered, grunted and turned.

There were nuts on the table. Kyle passed them to me. "I'm allergic," I said. Before Kyle could put the nuts down, Jane had already ordered a large nachos—"extra salsa, extra peppers."

Belushi was back before the next hurtin' song was over and didn't hesitate for a moment before depositing bottles in front of everyone including me. Each had a little slice of lime sticking out of the top. I watched as Kyle smoothly popped his lime into his bottle and I tried to poke mine in the same way. Naturally, my wedge stuck, so I discreetly pushed my finger right into the bottle hoping Jane wouldn't notice.

I'd tried wine a few times—if you could call the Manischewitz red my family served at Seder and Friday night dinners wine—and once, when I was on vacation in Honolulu and went to a party with some friends, had a pina colada and some brown cows because they tasted like liquid desserts. That was it for me and alcohol. But I was definitely having beer tonight, because Jane was buying beer.

"Here's what I'm thinking," Jane said. "You need to take this on the road. Tour Canada. Then, after that kicks ass, we tour the States."

Randy looked like he was choking on a nacho. "The United States?"

"Unless there are other states you'd like to tour," said Jane. "I think Australia has states."

Kyle was trying to picture himself onstage—in America. On Broadway. Then on screen. Robert Redford's career flashed before his eyes. "What do we have to do?"

Jane answered like she'd been plotting this for months, maybe years. "Make sure the show is portable. I like the music you used, but you'll need original tunes. That way we won't have any hassle over rights. And when we sell the soundtrack, we'll make all the money. And, obviously, we're looking at big illusions. Really big. Think you can do that?"

Norman nodded like this was his idea, then repeated the words with what almost passed for authority, "Original tunes."

"No problem," said Randy. "So we get a live band? That'll rock."

"No, better off with recorded music. Cheaper than having to pay a band every night. At least at first. I mean you do wanna make money off this, right?" She didn't have to wait for an answer—the dollar signs were already dancing in everyone's eyes like we were the cartoon nephews of Scrooge McDuck. "A band's expensive. So what you need's a soundtrack. You put together the show, I'll put together the tour. I was thinking we premiere here in August and start touring in September—you know, hit the campuses, build a following."

August?

August was only four months away.

A following?

"Groupies," said Randy.

Jane smiled. "Sure."

"So, you'll be our promoter?"

"Oh yeah," said cousin Jane.

Then, without warning, Randy produced a flower from the sleeve of his jacket, at least I was pretty sure it was from his sleeve. Jane laughed and clapped her hands lightly so just the table could hear her before Randy asked, "Can we share a trailer?"

Jane picked up her bottle but much to my surprise, not to hit him with it. "To *The Black Metal Fantasy.*"

We all clinked Coronas. I took my first sip of beer which tasted like flat, stale 7 Up, but it went down well with the jalapenos and the hurtin' tunes. I already felt drunk.

Original music. A tour. It wasn't exactly my fantasy life, but throw in a kiss from Sarah and it was darn close.

That's when reality sank in.

I was only a bit player here. Randy and Kyle and Lisa were the stars. Norman was the technician. And this was his cousin. I was just the hired help. The evil henchman.

Then Cousin Jane popped everyone else's balloons. "We need to do a showcase first. I need Brad to see what you can do." Brad. Brad Bowen. The man who ran Rainbow—the company that brought in acts like the Rolling Stones, the Who and the Bay City Rollers. And Randy thought performing for Cousin Jane was scary.

"So you want us to do the show again?" he asked.

Jane shook her head. "No." Her intensity surprised everyone.

"But you loved it," said Randy. "Won't Mr. Rainbow, Mr. Bowen, I mean Brad ..."

"No," she said before he could finish stammering his question. "I can see the potential here. But it's rough. Brad won't see how well you did that switch, he'll just see you're using bedsheets. He won't think about how you only need a bit of money to make a better guillotine. He'll just see this one's made out of wood. He'll eat you alive. You have to prove you can do something as good as ..." She fished for a moment, then landed the great white shark. "... Henning. So you need illusions like Henning's." She'd squished our dreams like they were a handful of Jacko's sponge balls.

None of us said anything, but nobody had to. There was no way we could make a show that looked like Henning's appear out of thin air. We were doomed. The only person who didn't look concerned was Jane.

"It's easy," she said.

Easy? "There's no way," said Randy.

Jane flashed that smile of hers again and this time it shone directly at Randy. "You don't have to do big illusions. Just do your best small ones. He doesn't need to see a full show. It's a showcase. Twenty minutes. You've got twenty minutes worth of good tricks, right?"

"No problem," said Randy.

"Great," said Jane. "Now that we're working together, I want to know what you're all about."

As another round of Coronas appeared, Jane stared at Randy, maybe through him. "So what are your ambitions?"

Randy didn't miss a beat. "Getting to know you better."

Jane was definitely looking through him. "You wanna be a star." It wasn't a question.

"Oh yeah," said Randy. Some things are too sacred to joke about.

She tilted her head and stared at Kyle. "And I know you wanna be a star."

Kyle smiled. I looked at the exit.

There was no way I was going to be part of a twenty-minute showcase.

Jane put her hand on mine. It was warm, I was warm—everywhere. "And what do you want?" I wanted to be smooth enough to give the same answer Randy just had.

"I don't bite," she smiled. It was definitely getting hotter at Bud's.

Somewhere, in some small part of my brain that she hadn't melted yet, I found the words. "I wanna be a writer."

Now she was looking through me.

"And what are you going to write?"

Before I could think about it, the words slipped out. "Something epic." I felt like an idiot.

Jane smiled, like she collected dreams the way I collected Batman comics and I'd given her a new one to slip into a protective plastic cover and hide away in the box in her closet. "So you should write the showcase."

Now Kyle chimed in. "That's a great idea."

Randy looked like his male ego had just been booted in the testicles.

"Yeah," said Lisa. "Mark's a real writer."

Suddenly, I had a bigger crush on Lisa than Randy did. I loved the way she said, "real writer."

Jane took her hand off mine and put it on Randy's. "You know, Randy, if Mark writes, you can focus on the magic."

"Yeah," he said, picking up Jane's thread. Then he turned to me. "You should write the script. But we'll work together on it. And you should direct, too. That way I don't have to worry about anything but the magic."

Wow. Suddenly I wasn't just involved, I was writing and directing a showcase for Rainbow Productions, a show that could tour the world. I definitely needed another beer. If I could only finish the first one. Even with the lime it tasted pretty gross.

"Can you have it ready in a month?"

This time Randy and I answered together. "No problem."

She lifted her bottle to toast. "Just remember to build this to tour. Because if it works, it's going everywhere." Then she repeated the last word so we'd hear it echoing in our dreams for years, maybe forever. "Everywhere."

7

The Dove Pan

We had a problem. We had a lot of problems. The biggest and best illusions we had were also the ones that looked the cheapest and tackiest if you got too close to the stage—and we had to assume the illustrious Brad Bowen was going to walk around our stage after the show and kick our magical tires. So the guillotine was out. We knew the Metamorphosis might work if we could borrow a nicer blanket and find a fancier helmet, but it didn't seem fair to ask Marvin to be part of the showcase, since he was too young to tour with the show.

Randy had a few ideas for big tricks he wanted to design, but he needed money and even though we knew we could get all the money in the world once Rainbow was on board, no one had any ideas for raising funds right away. Randy tried to borrow money from his mom, but she still hadn't forgiven him for ruining her favourite sheets.

No money, no Metamorphosis and no guillotine meant the only magic we could use to prove we could tour the world were birthday party tricks. How were we supposed to dazzle the great and powerful Brad by making sponge balls appear, conjuring cupcakes out of a "dove pan," spinning a few scarves around, and cutting and restoring rope?

While everyone else in my grad class was trying to do silly things like graduate, I was trying to figure out how to turn a handful of party tricks that could barely impress seven-year-olds into a magic spectacular that would dazzle the most important promoter I'd ever heard of. This all sounded exciting when Jane suggested it—but now it was terrifying. Every day at school whenever I wasn't searching for Sarah, Kyle seemed to be searching for me to ask if I'd figured out the script yet. A month? What was I thinking?

One night when I was supposed to be finishing several class projects, working on the school paper and learning my lines for the school play, I saw a used car ad on TV—or maybe it was a parody ad on *Saturday Night Live*—where the crazy salesman yelled at late-night viewers about how he could afford to make such impossible deals. His answer: "Volume, volume, volume."

The next day after school I asked Randy for a list of every illusion he owned, every illusion he could afford and every illusion he could fake. Then I got him to explain which ones took skill and which ones were all about gizmos and gimmicks. A general and particularly ironic rule of magic is that the smaller the trick, the tougher it usually is to do. It takes practice, coordination and skill to make a quarter vanish and pluck it from behind someone's ear. All it takes to make an elephant disappear is millions of quarters. If you can afford to buy the big illusions, you can do them. Most decent card tricks require weeks, months or even years of training to do well, never mind professionally. But all it takes to shoot fire is a fire-shooter, or well-placed flash pots and a guy like Norman sitting in the wings with a finger on the detonator. Once Randy and I broke down which tricks didn't require training I gave those to Kyle and Lisa, so everyone in the act could do something magical.

Then I condensed the story to cut down on the quest. Santar and Oryon would both do a bit of summoning, conjuring weapons in tricked-out versions of the tin that makes cupcakes appear—except instead of cracking eggs in it, they'd use fire. You can never go wrong with fire.

Doug Henning might have changed the face of magic, but he hadn't changed the pace. Most illusions Henning did were still presented with a big set-up, a flourish and a break for applause. If anyone else was doing an illusion or effect every minute, we hadn't seen them. And, if we were lucky, neither had Brad Bowen.

Once we had the script, we rehearsed the illusions for a couple of hours every day after school for three weeks. Because there was no Metamorphosis, there was no Adoma and that meant I got to watch from the audience with cousin Jane and Brad Bowen. When Jane walked in with Bowen she looked as nervous around him as we were around her. He wasn't a big guy, but he walked around like he was. He wore jeans and a fancy suit jacket and looked like important Hollywood people looked on TV shows.

The lights went down, then up. I watched Brad watch the showcase and his eyes were everywhere—taking in every illusion, examining studly Kyle, sexy Lisa and charming Randy.

Oryon and Santar met, monologued at each other, fired fire-shooters, flashed flash pots and, just when it looked like they were going to wreak havoc with a phenomenal Henning-level illusion … black out.

This was back when every girl in high school had a poster in her locker of a Bee Gee or a Wanna Bee Gee like Leif Garrett—who was the same age as Randy. After the set was over Brad didn't look at us, didn't talk to us, just stared, hands folded. We all watched, waited for … something … anything. Brad took in the onstage tableau one more time, then turned to Jane, muttered something and left without saying a word to any of us. It was obvious he hated it, until the auditorium door swung shut behind the man from Rainbow. Jane leapt to her feet, jumped on our stage and shrieked, "You're gonna be huge." It seemed crazy, but maybe it wasn't.

Randy hugged Lisa, Kyle hugged them both. I looked at Norman and we didn't hug, but we nodded to each other. It was official—we were gonna be huge.

"I can't wait to see the script for the real show," said Jane.

The real show ...

I barely had time to wonder if I was part of it when Randy turned to me. "So I guess we're writing that together, right, buddy?"

I was working on a real show ... for Rainbow. Screw graduation. Screw university. I'd made it. I was plotting my new life plan when I heard Jane add, "And we've gotta come up with a plan for your tour."

A plan ... I didn't have any idea what kind of plan Rainbow needed—none of us did—but as long as the point of the plan was fame, fortune and travelling North America with Lisa Jorgensen in skimpy costumes, we were in. After Jane left to meet Brad, the rest of us sat on the stage, basking in the residual magic.

The next night, I visited Randy's apartment for the first time. A few months earlier Randy had found a job and moved out of his mom's basement. He was working for the one employer in the world who would never notice or care if he came to work stoned, or occasionally called in sick to work on a magic show—the federal government. Thanks to a friend of his mother's he'd scored a clerical job, something to do with printing Unemployment Insurance cheques. He was still performing magic for parties, benefits and special events, but as good as he was, there wasn't enough of a nightclub scene in the city for magic tricks to pay the bills for much more than buying more magic tricks. But *The Black Metal Fantasy* was a chance to change that.

With the money from the new government job, Randy rented a bachelor pad on Broadway—a generic commercial strip that was starting to move upscale as older apartment blocks were being knocked down to create new stores and office complexes, so Randy's building was destined for the wrecking ball.

You could smell Randy's place from the hall. It smelled like ... happy skunks. And disinfectant. And something else I didn't recognize. I sniffed again when we stepped inside. "What's burning?" It smelled sort of like ... flowers.

"Incense," said Randy. I nodded sagely or perhaps patchoul-y, like I knew what incense was.

Randy's bedroom had black light posters and dirtier porn magazines than I'd ever seen before. *Playboy* was risqué, *Penthouse* was raunchy, but *Hustler* was ... the women in there scared me. Not only did none of them look like Sarah, they looked like if they met Sarah on the street they'd beat her up and steal her stuff.

I followed the bass line of *Dark Side of the Moon* into a living room that was basically a couch bed, a few tables, a stereo, a TV with a flaming red skull candle perched on top of it, and stacks of abandoned takeout food containers.

I started pacing in circles while Randy sucked on something that looked like a small blue aquarium designed to drive fish crazy. Then he offered the fish tank to me. I shook my head, he shrugged, sucked on it again, coughed, and tried to figure out what we'd do for the big show.

After the album was over and the only profound thought we came up with was that we needed another hot girl or two in the cast, Randy wanted a snack, so we decided to walk four blocks to the nearest 7-Eleven. Randy grabbed a big bag of neon orange-coloured cheese things. I tossed in a few quarters to feed my addiction and grabbed a Coke Slurpee. "We wanna be like *Star Wars* on stage," I said as we walked back to the apartment.

"Bigger than *Star Wars*," said Randy. "If this works it won't just be a play, we'll do the movie and then ..."

I knew where he was going and I was already there, dreaming of coloured panels and glossy covers illustrated by Neal Adams, picturing the awesome cover of *X-Men 59* with Cyclops standing alone against the Sentinels. "Comic books," said Randy. And for the first time I knew we were soulmates. "*Heavy Metal* comic books."

Okay, maybe not total soulmates. I preferred Marvel, or even DC, but sure, *Heavy Metal* would work.

"And cartoons."

"Cartoons would be cool. I love cartoons."

"So it's not just a story," I said.

"It's an epic," said Randy.

The next idea was mine. I wish it had been Randy's, I really do, but it was mine. I was obsessed with *The Lord of the Rings*. George Lucas had announced that *Star Wars* was going to be a trilogy, too—maybe even a modern epic. And I'd just studied classical epics in English Lit. We were learning about Dante's *Inferno*, so I knew proper epics were nine parts. They started *in medias res*—which was either Latin or English Lit for "in the middle of the story." Nine parts. That's why Lucas had labelled the first film in his *Star Wars* saga "Episode IV." So maybe it wasn't my fault. Maybe we should blame Lucas for convincing us that every great story had to be part of a trilogy, which meant our story had to be part of a trilogy. Yes, I absolutely blame George Lucas and his damned Jedi mind-tricks for the fact that the next words out of my mouth were "Let's make it a trilogy!"

Randy loved the idea.

I loved the idea.

It was brilliant. It was obvious. If we were gonna be huge—if we were going to be the next *Star Wars* or *Lord of the Rings* and create a new mythology that would take over the world, it had to be a trilogy.

"So we know the ending," I said. Every trilogy has the same ending. The final battle. The end of the quest. Good versus evil for control of The Force, the fate of the Shire, all the cosmic marbles. "But what's part one?"

"Oryon's story."

"Oryon's story. Cool." I said "cool" a lot. I still say cool a lot. "What about Kyle?"

"He can be in it. We'll need a few scenes with Santar—to set up episode two." We went back to Randy's place, he started rolling a joint, and I started pacing in circles again and asked Randy what Oryon's story was.

"I dunno," he said. "You're the writer."

For the showcase I didn't have to worry much about plot, never mind character motivations, but to tell the whole story I needed to know the history of Medemptia and the origins of all our heroes and villains. Every hero needs an amazing secret origin story. But the less Randy gave me, the more fun I could have making it up myself. It was time to find out what I had to work with. "Let's start with the magic," I said. This time instead of asking for a list of all the tricks he had, I asked what tricks he always wanted to do, what we could build, what we could buy. "What's the coolest stuff we can do?"

"Pretty much anything if we've got enough money. I've got some wild ideas. Stuff nobody's ever seen before." Randy started scrawling on a legal pad. I started pacing, trying to imagine the coolest trick in the world.

A few minutes later Randy passed me his notes. Then Randy lit his joint and was about to put it to his lips, when he stopped himself and offered it to me.

"That's okay," I said, waving him away.

"You sure you don't want some?"

I shook my head.

"It'll help you write."

"It's okay," I said again.

"No problem," said Randy. "More for me." Randy inhaled, coughed, smiled.

"What's the coolest trick you can imagine?" asked Randy.

I'd always loved escapes. When I first learned magic I'd practised with ropes and locks and handcuffs. I'd practised twisting my wrists so that if anyone ever put me in handcuffs or tied my wrists I'd be free in seconds. I knew about Houdini's water escapes, the tricks Houdin did to convince a tribe in Africa that he was a God and pretty much everything Henning had ever done, but I'd never tried to dream up new illusions before.

Randy tried to help me by breaking down the basics. "There are really only a few tricks—appearances, disappearances, levitations, escapes, psychic stuff—everything else is pretty much a variation on the theme." He'd scrawled down his favourites and decorated them with hand-drawn stars and lightning bolts. The more lightning bolts, the more he liked the trick.

Levitation.

Decapitation.

Walking through a mirror.

Transformation.

Fire appearance.

I could already picture the effects—and the audience's reaction. "You can really do all this?"

"No problem."

"Cool."

"You sure you don't want some?" Randy offered the joint again.

"No thanks."

"How are you supposed to write this without drugs? I was stoned the whole time I wrote the first script."

That explained a lot.

"I always figured you for a major stoner," he said.

Everybody did. One night I'd been working late on the student paper and everybody started sharing their most humiliating drug experiences. Even our sponsor teacher joined in, talking about the time in college when she tried LSD, climbed on the roof of her apartment and was convinced she could fly. After everyone else told their stories, they turned to me. I was the editor. I had to have a story. A great story. "I've never tried drugs," I said. Everyone laughed—including my sponsor.

"It's okay," she said, "I'm not going to narc on you."

I didn't know what to say, so I said nothing and my sponsor shook her head, like I'd betrayed her. She'd trusted me with her story about trying to fly off a building and here I was claiming I'd never smoked a joint.

I had no problem with the idea of marijuana.

I didn't get why it was illegal since pretty much everybody I'd ever met had tried it and I'd never seen anyone pick a fight because they'd had too much dope. But since I'd started high school everyone—friends, teachers, even family—assumed I was taking drugs because of my writing. One reason for this was that I loved stoner humour like *Saturday Night Live* and *National Lampoon*, but I had no clue it was stoner humour. I wrote stories about potato chips laced with micro-chips created to take over the world. I once brought a potato into class with a plug sticking out of it and declared it, "the electric potato"—it could do everything a regular potato could do AND it was electric. My other fake products included such absurd concepts as shell-less eggs and caffeine-free cola. "If they can put a man on the moon, why can't they make a cola without caffeine."

I also used to buy postcards wherever I went and filled them out as if I was an alien tourist. Then I'd send them to my favourite writing teacher (who I'd address as Xonthar), list all the beautiful sites I'd seen ... and disintegrated.

And since that was my idea of funny, and this was Vangroovy, every time people read one of my stories they'd ask, "What were you on when you wrote it?"

I was proud of my imagination and the idea that people thought it wasn't my imagination, that it was some combination of chemicals spinning my synapses, really offended me. I decided that as long as I was going to be a writer I was never going to do drugs. If I had an idea, I wanted to make sure it was mine. So the strongest drug I regularly ingested while writing was my ever-present Coke.

"You're the writer, what do you want to do now?" It was a question, but it was also a challenge. Maybe Randy didn't need me. Maybe he could write this himself or bring in another writer, someone with a wild, drug-fueled imagination or ...

I tried to imagine the world's coolest trick, something amazing, something impossible. And as I stared at the burning skull candle I knew what we had to do.

"Set the audience on fire."

Randy almost dropped his joint. "What?"

"Wouldn't that be the coolest trick ever?"

"Burning down the theatre?"

"Not burning down the theatre. Lighting the audience on fire. But not for real—just making them think they're on fire. Wouldn't that be the ultimate illusion? It's always about getting the magician in trouble, right? Making them think the magician's gonna die. The ultimate—that's gotta be scaring the hell out of the audience. Making them think they're gonna die. That would be the coolest trick ever."

Randy stared at me. "Yeah."

"So you can't do it?" I laughed. Randy wasn't laughing though. The fire sparked something.

"I think you're right. Let's do something to the audience. We can't set them on fire but ..."

Now he stared at the skull candle, focusing. It was like he was talking to the skull, not me, when he continued. "We can make an audience member vanish. What about that?"

It wasn't perfect, but as Randy said it, I realized we were onto something, something amazing. Maybe not the coolest trick ever, but really cool. "I got it," I said. "Why not kill someone?"

Randy grinned.

I started to pace again, full speed. "We grab someone, kidnap them or hypnotize them or whatever and we bring them onstage and kill them. Light them on fire, cut them in half, put them in the guillotine, whatever, but we kill them. That'll freak everybody out."

"You want to kill an audience member?"

"Yeah!" I was pacing so fast I was practically jogging. "That'd be cool. But maybe it doesn't have to be a real audience member. We can ..."

"A plant?" Now he jumped off the couch and started to pace too.

"Yeah. But nobody will know it's a plant. When we grab our victim, they'll freak, they'll scream. In a real magic show people volunteer, right? But this isn't a real magic show—we're in a demon dimension.

So what if we grab someone and they try to make a run for it. And then ..."

"We kill them."

"Exactly."

"Can we do it?" I asked.

"If it's a plant."

"Can we light them on fire?"

"We'd need a lot of mirrors."

"Sounds expensive."

"Too expensive." Then, "We could do a vanish!"

"No," I said, and I was completely sure of myself now. "They've got to die. Onstage. You always see the magician or the assistant do the life and death stuff. And all the volunteer guy from the audience ever does is check the chains, or hold a stopwatch, or something boring. I want the person from the audience to be the one in chains. And since they're not part of the show, once we kill them, we leave them dead. Let them bleed all over the place. Let the audience wonder what really happened. We won't even let them take a curtain call, won't let them leave the theatre till everyone's gone. I mean the audience probably won't fall for it, but maybe ..." And I grinned.

We were going to kill an audience member. That would be cool.

"You're right," said Randy as he stubbed out the remains of his joint. "You don't need drugs."

8

Happy Phase

Dr. Bob was my best friend by accident. He wasn't a doctor, but I was sure he would be one day—unless I had already destroyed his medical career. And there was a character on *The Muppet Show* named "Doctor Bob," so that's what I called him.

Bob had transferred from a school in Montreal just before starting grade eleven, and he arrived a week late. That meant when he started in chemistry class, Bob didn't know anyone else there, so he got stuck with me as a lab partner. Science and I didn't get along. The chemistry teacher and I got along even worse. Even though I was only in grade ten I was in grade eleven chem because I'd taken an advanced-credit science class in summer school as an excuse to hang out with Sarah, but since Sarah was in the class—which was the whole point of taking it—none of the science stuck.

I'd destroyed any chance of decent grades during our second week when our very proper teacher, Mr. Joaquin, was trying to explain the difference between animate and inanimate objects. He wanted to make sure we knew that living creatures all shared similar traits. The ones I still remember (and I hope Mr. Joaquin is impressed that something he taught me stuck) is they could eat, excrete and reproduce.

After telling us all we needed to know the definition of life, our teacher turned to us and asked, "And how do we know that a candle isn't alive?"

My hand shot up.

"Because it doesn't scream when you light it on fire!"

All the students laughed.

Mr. Joaquin suggested I move to the empty table at the back of the class, and that was where Dr. Bob found me when he arrived. When he asked to pair up with me for an assignment, I should have warned him to run—but I didn't know he had dreams of doing cutting-edge, real-world research.

When Bob showed me the screaming candle he'd doodled in his notebook I suggested we hand in one of our assignments in a series of cartoon panels, like a comic book. It was on cell multiplication. Don't ask me why we were doing cell multiplication in chem class. Bob drew all the different phases of cell development. We had all the right phases, but we added a bonus answer. At my urging, Bob drew one of the cells grinning demonically and we labelled that last one, "Happy Phase."

Thanks to Bob I passed the class. Barely.

Thanks to me, my new friend the science whiz passed the class, too—with a C+. But Bob liked my sense of humour and I liked that he'd had a life outside of school. He'd travelled. He'd lived in America and Quebec. He even spoke French. By the time I realized he was a jock (a sprinter and basketball player) and he discovered I was a geek (acting in school plays and running the school paper), it was too late, we were already friends, even though I was a grade below him and two years younger.

That summer after grade ten (grade eleven for Bob) we went backpacking across Canada together. I was supposed to be going with a dozen friends from my grade. We'd been planning the trip for months. It was a few weeks before the end of the school year and time to book the Via Rail passes when an invisible blizzard hit, giving everyone else cold feet. The idea was to travel across the country for a month on less than a thousand dollars each, and none of my friends liked my suggestion that we stay in youth hostels. They were scared of them, or their parents wouldn't allow them to go, or they were scared of them so they claimed their parents wouldn't allow them to go. Brett, the last of my would-be travelling companions, a train buff with a basement filled with models and a track he'd been building since he was six, told me he'd go with me. "But I won't get off the train." Brett wanted to take a real-life train ride, but he just wanted to go all the way from Vancouver to Halifax and back.

I was so upset I left the history classroom where my wouldn't-be travelling companions were eating lunch and retreated to the cafeteria to drown my sorrows in a burnt egg roll with plum sauce. Dr. Bob saw me. "What's wrong?"

I was too upset to explain, so I snapped at him instead. "You wanna go across Canada with me?"

He didn't miss a beat. "Sure," he said. That night I went to his house for the first time and he played *Blood on the Tracks*. I'd heard of Bob Dylan, but as far as I was aware I'd never heard him before. I listened to seventies rock radio—which was cool at the time since, hey, it was the seventies, and the alternative was disco dudes in pants so tight they made 'em sing like a castrati. This would be my way of saying ... not a Bee Gees fan. When I discovered the worst singing voice I'd ever heard belonged to THE legend of the sixties all I could think of was, "they really were stoned all the time, weren't they." I told Bob I thought Dylan's voice sounded like gravel being sucked up by a vacuum. He looked at me like he was channelling Mr. Joaquin. But he still agreed to go across Canada with me.

Then he turned me onto Frank Zappa and Arlo Guthrie.

A month later we took trains, ferries and buses, and hitchhiked through every province but New Brunswick. We stepped onto the station platform at Moncton, thought it was too ugly, and got back on the train. We stayed in youth hostels every night—and every night when I handed over my ID the person running the hostel phoned the RCMP to make sure I wasn't a runaway, or a kidnap victim. I was still sixteen. Bob was eighteen.

We saw lobster fishermen in Newfoundland, the Anne of Green Gables House, the Anne of Green Gables musical, the wall around Quebec City, Parliament Hill, the CN Tower, Maple Leaf Gardens, the Sudbury Big Nickel, Saskatchewan's alleged mountain and—special bonus sightseeing highlight—a naked woman who stepped over me one night when she thought I was asleep in the Charlottetown Youth Hostel.

So Dr. Bob was definitely open to my crazy ideas. But when he heard about *The Black Metal Fantasy* he didn't get it. "You're already doing school plays."

"But this is real."

Bob wasn't sold. Then he saw the show at the JCC. And he saw Lisa in the harem outfit. And cousin Jane. Bob was in university. He was almost the same age as Jane. "Maybe I can help."

"Sure," I said. "That would be great." I knew we'd need help. I just didn't know what kind, or how much. When Bob came to my house a few nights after the showcase I was in my room trying to figure out our story. I had a manual typewriter and all the vital posters on my bedroom wall: Spider-Man, Batman, the wickedly cool Bakshi *Lord of the Rings* fellowship with Gandalf front and centre, and an illustrated *Star Wars*, with Luke and Leia striking heroic poses, that I'd bought from the Comic Shop for a then-astronomical sum of seven dollars. My record player was playing the only album I ever played when I worked: *Bat Out of Hell* by Meat Loaf. Awesome lyrics by Jim Steinman. It was an album I first heard on my cross-country trip with Dr. Bob when we were in a car with two friendly nursing students from Regina, one of whom might have been a lot friendlier to me if I'd been clever enough to lie about my age.

Bob was not amused to see me working. "We're gonna miss the movie."

"Sorry, just a few more pages."

Bob collapsed on my couch.

A few years earlier when my mom was redecorating I saw a desk I loved—a modern reproduction of a classic nineteenth-century roll-top. It was a writer's desk and I wanted it desperately. My mom said I couldn't have it, because it was too big for my room. "If you get a desk that big you won't have any space for a bed."

The answer was obvious. "So I won't have a bed."

I gave my bed to my brother David, and mom bought me a cheap, brown fold-out couch. I thought it should be brown because the desk was brown and besides, brown wouldn't show dirt. Some nights I'd pull the couch bed open to sleep, but most nights I'd sleep on the couch cushions. I was a writer and had a writer's desk—who needed a bed? "I don't get why you're doing this," said Bob. "It's your last summer before university."

I didn't look up, just kept hitting the keys. "I'm getting to write a real play."

"Does *Sarah* like magic?" Bob said the name singsong style. I hadn't told him. I knew I hadn't told him. How did he know?

He smiled at me like the lost cause I was. "Everything you do is about Sarah."

I stared at my typewriter more intently—like I was thinking about something particularly deep. "Not everything."

"So she'll come to the show and fall for Randy. Or Kyle."

He was wrong. He had to be wrong. "I could do something really great here."

"Like see *Alien*," he reminded me. "It's supposed to be really scary."

"Yeah, a scary science-fiction movie. Right."

"You know what'll be scary?"

I turned away from the typewriter. If this was another joke about Sarah I was going to hit him.

"Rafting."

Rafting?

"We should go whitewater rafting. Everybody at the lab's going." Bob's dad was a research scientist at St. Paul's Hospital and Bob worked at the lab, cleaning up monkey droppings and doing odd jobs.

"*Everyone?*" I asked, with the same tone he'd asked about Sarah. "Even Cecillllle?"

"Shut up." Yup, Cecile was definitely going. She worked in the lab, but as far as I knew, she hadn't talked to him yet, or acknowledged his existence. "It's only a hundred bucks. And we get to spend the night camping, we get dinner and breakfast and lunch the next day and then it's three hours, right around Hell's Gate. It'll be fun."

Fun. I pictured falling out of the raft, landing in a whirlpool and screaming for the rescuers who would shout back from the shore, "The water's too rough," before watching us go under for the third time. "And you think this is crazy?"

"So you wanna go?"

"Not really."

"So let's at least see the movie," he said. "If we're gonna catch the trailers we've gotta go now.

"There's no way a sci-fi movie's gonna be scary."

If only that was my worst prediction of the year.

9

The Trilogy

Randy was a hardcore horror fan. I was convinced he'd read every-thing Stephen King had even thought of writing. He'd seen every horror movie I'd ever heard of and hundreds I hadn't. He had stacks of paperback books with black covers and ominous raised red or silver letters spelling out titles that included every possible variation on the words *darkness*, *death*, *nightmare*, *evil* and *terror*.

I loved superheroes. I owned more than ten thousand comics— *Justice League*, *X-Men*, *The Avengers*, *The Teen Titans*, *Batman*, *Spider-Man*, *Daredevil*, *Green Lantern*, *Flash*, *Aquaman*, *Nova*, *Hulk*, *Moon Knight*, *Howard the Duck* ... When I read books for fun it was mostly sci-fi or ideally, sci-fi humour like Kurt Vonnegut or Douglas Adams.

I'd never been into Conan, so I had no idea that's where Randy pulled most of his mythology and terminology from. I didn't realize Medemptia sounded a lot like Conan's hometown of Cimmeria. I'd seen *Conan* comics, but they looked dumber than "Hulk mad, Hulk smash!" So I assumed Santar's helmet was inspired by Norse mythol-ogy, not Robert E. Howard's. I wouldn't realize until years later that any character or place name in Randy's script that wasn't from Conan was lifted from *Battlestar Galactica*.

It turned out Randy had invented just enough mythology for the first show to string together the tricks and create a scenario where two guys got to fight over Lisa. But that didn't matter. What mattered was that if there was going to be a great battle we had to figure out what it was about, who was in it and why everybody was fighting. Since we were creating a trilogy, we had to dream up two big stories that took place before the fighting started.

It was Kyle who established the first major flaw in the plan. He loved the idea of a trilogy. "Every major story has to be part of a trilogy," said Kyle. But as soon as we told him how it started ... "I'm not doing it."

Randy and I were floored.

"Oryon's story? You want me to spend all summer rehearsing so I can go on tour with Oryon's story?"

"You'll be in it, you'll be ..."

Randy and I took turns pleading.

There was a perfect solution, an obvious solution.

"Why not Santar's story?" he suggested.

That was not it.

The correct answer, for those of you playing at home, would have been: DON'T DO A TRILOGY. DO A BETTER VERSION OF THE SHOW THAT DAZZLED JANE AND FOUR HUNDRED PEOPLE.

None of us even considered the correct answer. Instead, Kyle started making his case. "You have to introduce the villain first. So you know what the hero's up against."

I knew this had nothing to do with storytelling. Kyle wanted to be the star. But Randy was the magician. *The Black Metal Fantasy* was his baby. He was the guy who should be front and centre in the first show and ...

"No problem," said Randy. "The second show will be all about Oryon."

"Great," said Kyle.

I would have bet my entire comic collection that if the second show was all about Oryon, Kyle was not going to be there for it. But it never crossed Randy's mind that there wouldn't be three shows and he had no doubt that after the first one we'd be so big, Kyle would never consider walking away from the sequel. So part one was going to be about Santar.

As the writer, I loved the idea. Villains are more fun. We'd already established the relationship between Santar and Gamatria. And Randy, or Oryon, would still be in the show. Somehow. But the focus would be on Santar, aka Kyle.

"I'll be designing all the magic," Randy told me. "Even if I'm not onstage that much, it's all about the magic. I'll still be the star."

It was time to start putting together "Episode One." Or maybe, "Episode Four: A New Hope." We needed to know how much money we had.

Randy was determined to have a character emerge from a mirror, and he figured that trick alone would cost at least two thousand dollars to build. He tried to explain how it was done, but I was less interested in how it was done than how cool it would look when we did it. It's another trick that was eventually used in *Phantom of the Opera*. If the Phantom's secret identity had been Santar, we would have had to investigate whether Andrew Lloyd Webber had tapped our phones.

"Do you think Rainbow is going to pay for all this?" I asked.

"They don't have to," he said, an even bigger grin than usual spreading across his face. "We have an investor."

"An investor? Who is it?"

"That's a secret," said Randy. "For now."

10

Su Casa

While everyone else in grade twelve was dreaming of graduation day, I was dreaming of *The Black Metal Fantasy*. My grad gift was going to be fame and fortune. Dr. Bob was wrong. My parents didn't tell me I was crazy. They just told me if I wanted to do "that magic show," I had to get a summer job and pay my own bills. They also weren't keen on me coming home at 3 a.m. every night and waking everybody up.

I already had a part-time job, but it didn't pay much. I was a freelance gorilla. Sometimes I was a bunny rabbit. Occasionally I was a reindeer. I'll explain later.

I had a few thousand dollars in savings and I could make more by selling off some of the gems from my comic collection—if I unloaded all my *X-Men*s and *Spider-Man*s. There was no way I could sell my *Batman*s or *Justice League*s or *Brave and the Bold*s 28, 29 and 30 featuring the first appearances of the Justice League. I'd sell a kidney first. But ...

Kyle, Randy and I were at Bud's to brainstorm possible tricks. I wanted to order a Coke, but Kyle told me that would get us all ID'd so he suggested apple cider. "It's okay if you nurse a cider all night.

Nursing a beer ... that's just disturbing." When the nachos arrived I told them the bad news. "I can't afford to do this. I need a summer job or I can't really live at home."

"But we're gonna be rich," said Randy.

"I don't have the money. I can't do it. You have a job."

"Just ask our investor for enough money so we can pay him," suggested Kyle.

Pay? That would work. That would be great. "Could we?" I asked Randy. "Maybe I could meet him. Or her. Or them."

Randy had another brainstorm. "Move in with me."

Move in with Randy? Move out of the house? Move in with Randy?

"But I don't have a job. I can't afford it."

"I'll pay the rent. That'll be my investment."

"You're kidding," said Kyle.

I was glad he said it. I was still trying to come up with a response.

"Why not? Move in for the summer. After that we're going on tour anyway, right? Your folks will love it. Besides, then I get my own driver." Randy not only didn't have a car, he'd never learned to drive. "Never wanted to," said Randy. "I always worried I'd be too easily ..." And his eyes were on Bud's new waitress. When she vanished into the kitchen he continued. "And ya know what'll also be a lot easier at my place than your parents'?"

I knew there was a correct answer to this one. "Coming home at 3 a.m.?"

"Coming home at 3 a.m. with a girl." As soon as I heard Randy say it, I knew that was a much better answer than mine. And I knew that by getting it wrong ...

Randy examined me like I'd been plopped down by a twister in the middle of the Yellow Brick Road. "You're a ...."

"No way," said Kyle.

The most action I'd ever gotten was a brief diplomatic liaison with the Ambassador from France when I was my school's delegate to a model UN in grade eleven and the French delegate and I snuck outside where she demonstrated her country's national form of kissing with me. I was the ambassador from Morocco. My qualification: ... I'd seen *Casablanca* three times. We went for a walk in Stanley Park that ended with us lying in the grass on a secluded path where she let me slide my hands under her halter top and touch her seins before she returned to her real home in the wilds of Saskatchewan. So until now, "getting laid," hadn't interested me as much as getting to first base. Or finding out where the bases were. Or being invited to see the diamond.

This had never been a big deal before. Except for Dr. Bob, all my friends were geekier than I was. But now ... The best I could hope for was their laughter would be merciless. The worst... They'd be afraid my virginity might be contagious, that I was too much of a loser to join their reindeer games. I tried to come up with something to defuse the situation, to defend myself, to ...

"Don't worry," said Randy. "Your Uncle Randy will fix that." And he smiled—but he didn't laugh. Neither did Kyle.

The next night I arrived at Randy's, dragged in my backpack and a garbage bag full of clothes, and Randy led me to the front room and pointed at the couch covered with magazines, pizza boxes, empty beer cans littered with mysterious metal clips and small cardboard matchbox things that used to hold something called Zig-Zags. "This is your bed," he said. He removed the bong from it. "And this is your room."

"Cool," I said. I'd never had a room before—not in a real apartment.

I moved the bong off the bong table (that table had never met coffee) took my typewriter out of my pack and set it up on top of the *Yellow Pages*. There was no desk—definitely no authentic rolltop writer's desk.

"You can write on the kitchen table," he said.

"I can?"

"*Mi casa es su casa.*"

I stared at him blankly. I'd failed French.

"It'll be great to have a roomie. I don't cook. Do you cook?"

After barely surviving shop class I'd transferred to home ec because it seemed like cooking would come in a lot handier in real life than learning how to build a birdhouse, so I knew how to cook a few things. I thought I'd be the only guy in class and have to deal with a lot of abuse, but fortunately the two other guys studying cooking were the same guys who were in playwriting and directing with me—the school's toughest delinquent, and the captain, or quarterback, or whatever you call the biggest, baddest guy on the rugby team. The few times someone questioned my masculinity because I was learning to quiche I suggested I'd share their thoughts on the culinary arts with the other guys in the class. When I revealed who my fellow chefs were the apologies weren't just desperate, but tearful. Anyway, I knew how to cook—at least by guy standards circa 1980. This was gonna be great.

"Only one rule. If you've got company and don't want to be interrupted, leave a hanger on the doorknob."

"What for?"

"So I don't interrupt you."

It took me a moment to realize what he thought he might be interrupting, besides my writing. Then ... I did. And then, nope, I still couldn't imagine it being an issue. "Sure ... so what if I come home and there's a hanger?"

Randy grinned. "There's a Denny's down the street. Open all night."

This didn't sound good. "So I spend the whole night at Denny's?"

"I won't leave the hanger out all night." Then he grinned conspiratorially. "Not that I couldn't."

I smiled conspiratorially like I knew exactly what he was talking about.

"If anything isn't where you put it, don't freak out, it's probably the poltergeist."

"We've got a poltergeist? Is it dangerous?"

"No, it just move things around. You can tell when its been around because usually when something is missing, it smells a bit like lemon afterwards. I call him "Lemon Scented Poultry.""

Everybody knew poltergeists had a strange citrusy smell, at least everybody who read the same horror comics I did.

The place was haunted? We were in a haunted apartment?

It really was perfect.

||

The Near Assassination of Little Bunny Foo Foo

Some people have skeletons in their closets—I have large, furry cartoon animals. I'd been the Easter Bunny. I'd also been a bear, a gorilla, two different kinds of chicken, a valentine, a reindeer and Frosty the Snowman. I had a part-time job with a company that provided singing telegrams and costumed entertainers for special events.

I'd delivered a bouquet of helium balloons to a pair of newlyweds on the church steps. I was dressed as an eight-foot-tall bunny.

While working as a bear I'd greeted a group of Russian tourists whose ship was stranded in dry dock—a dry dock they couldn't leave in case they tried to defect.

And I'd once spent half an hour in the men's room of a fancy downtown restaurant wearing a propeller beanie, white slacks and a lime-green vest and holding a batch of balloons as I waited for the maître d' to track down the man I was supposed to serenade with *Happy Birthday*.

The first time I'd showed up at the office for Big One Fantasy— no relation to *Black Metal Fantasy*—it was filled with the usual office equipment—desks, typewriters, filing cabinets, propeller beanies, huge animal heads and helium tanks. I'd read an ad in the paper and come for a job interview, but the guy behind the desk, who looked and sounded vaguely like a young Jimmy Cagney, checked my height the same way Kyle had, asked my name and as soon as I said, "Mark," asked if I'd ever been a gorilla before.

I hadn't.

He said he needed a gorilla downtown in thirty minutes, then pointed me toward the suit, said, "This is what gorillas do" and proceeded to jump around the room, make an assortment of rude noises and hug me. "You can also sniff people's pant legs. People go crazy when you sniff their pant legs." I could understand that. "And if you see a bald guy, rub his head. Always good for a laugh. Just don't talk. Gorillas don't talk."

"I see," I said.

"Then you sing *Happy Birthday*."

"But I don't talk?"

"Never." Cagney saw no contradiction. "Your job is to sing *Happy Birthday* to Gary. Here's the hotel, they're in the conference room. Be there in twenty minutes. Your name is Gus. My name is Cal."

His name was Cal, my name was Gus, and I was a gorilla bounding toward a downtown hotel conference room holding a bouquet of multicoloured helium balloons for Gary.

I sniffed pants. People did go crazy. I jumped around, picked up plates, took the glasses from a bald guy and tried them on, then replaced them on the top of his head. I jumped on chairs, howled, screeched and, of course, sang, *Happy Birthday* to Gary in a raspy, guttural voice. Gary was thoroughly humiliated. It was a job well done.

By the time I got back to the Big One Fantasy office, Cal had realized I wasn't the Mark he was looking for. The other Mark—an experienced gorilla—had shown up a few minutes after I left with the costume. I discovered when I returned the costume that Cal had just made the jump from "talent" to running the office and hadn't met the other performers yet. I'd broken into showbiz by mistake and now I was a star.

A few weeks later I did my first bunny gig. The moment I saw the ratty grey fur, huge ears, buckteeth and sweater painted like a Ukrainian Easter egg I was in love. "This is how bunny talks," Cal said, doing his high-pitched bunny voice. For those of you who've never been, or met, an eight-foot-tall rabbit, Bunny sounded like a precocious six-year-old sitcom kid.

Cal taught me the bunny song. "Little Bunny Foo Foo running froo da forest, catches all da field mice, bops 'em on da heads."

I repeated the lyrics.

"It's actually "chops off all their heads," said Cal, "but that makes some of the little kids cry, so this is our official Big One Fantasy version."

My first bunny job was at an upscale high-rise in suburbia. The victim was an uptight young lawyer and I was his girlfriend's idea of a present. When I arrived, Perry Mason tried to humiliate me.

Never engage in a battle of the wits with an eight-foot-tall rabbit—or a seven-foot-tall chicken or bear. There's no way to make a guy in a funny animal costume seem more foolish than he looks and you come across as stupid for taking the big bunny, bear or bird seriously. When Perry called me a "freak," I explained that I'd eaten a nuclear carrot. Bunnies could talk all they liked.

A macho grocery clerk got bunny for his birthday, took me to his favourite bar and complained to anyone who would listen, "I told my wife I wanted a *Playboy* bunny."

Bunny's high-pitched reply: "I am a playboy. Bring on the chicks."

On my second job as a gorilla I sang *Happy Birthday* to a guy named Chuck. Chuck and his girlfriend had obviously been celebrating for some time and were convinced I was their friend Mitch. "C'mon Mitch," Chuck kept saying, "take off your mask." I growled and started for the door. The pair chased me all around the room.

Chuck tackled me, but I was holding onto my mask for dear life. His girlfriend tickled my armpits. I let go and off came the mask. The pair were shocked into sobriety when they saw that I wasn't Mitch, but they were even more startled when I let out a howl like a wounded gorilla and pulled the mask back over my head. Their laughter was replaced by soft-spoken apologies.

"Would you like a drink?" Chuck asked. "Scotch maybe?"

I nodded, then growled. I'd never had Scotch.

He poured me a Scotch. "You can take off your mask if you like."

I shook my head to indicate the mask wasn't moving and then said, in my gorilla singing voice, "Shraw."

"What?"

"Shraw." Chuck fished through his cupboard, then handed me a straw. I sipped my Scotch through the mask, growled my thanks, stumbled out the door and took off my costume a few blocks away.

I almost got into fights whenever I was dressed as a chicken. Kids like to kick chickens.

But the Easter Bunny has enemies, too. I was working at a down-scale mall dressed as a big fluffy white rabbit and I had a job to do. I sat in my throne with a basket of chocolate eggs in one paw. I felt like Santa Claus and, just like Santa, I was poked, pinched, prodded and squealed at. A few of the tots would take one look at me and start to bawl uncontrollably. I could always see it coming. Their lower lip would start to quiver. Professionals can spot these things. If you're ever dressed as the Easter Bunny and you see a kid's lower lip start to quiver, back off. I'd often spot this telltale sign and warn the parents—"I think she's a little scared, maybe you'd better ..."—and they'd take that as their cue to thrust the terrified toddler right at me. Maybe they liked scaring their kids?

In between kids sitting on my lap, I waved at shoppers. After about an hour I waved at one surly dude in a ball cap and he stopped, stared at me and made a slashing gesture across his throat. Then he came close enough for me to hear him whisper, "You're dead meat."

All I could think of was, "I'll bet this never happens to Santa Claus." I probably would have forgotten the whole thing if not for the fact that three hours later—five minutes before closing time—the guy came back and made the same gesture and mouthed the same words.

I admit I was one scared bunny.

I didn't get paid enough to risk being turned into rabbit stew. I hopped over to the information desk and had them page security. When the guard showed up I told him my story. As he escorted me to my car the guard did an incredible job of keeping a straight face. I imagined the story that would run in the papers the next day if my stalker found me. "Easter Bunny Slain—Chicken Little in Custody."

And as I stripped off my fur, tucked my rabbit ears into the trunk of my little Honda Civic and drove off into the sunset I pictured the attacker in court, pleading before the jurors—"The rabbit deserved it. I never got no Easter eggs when I was a kid."

My most dangerous moment on the job was a birthday party gig.

Dr. Bob and I had tickets to a Canucks game, but Cal had said I could take the gig as long as I showed up at the house before midnight. At eleven—after the Canucks lost another heartbreaker—I approached the neighbourhood and discovered the power was out. Even the traffic lights were gone. Mom was waiting outside. It was her little girl's "sweet sixteen" party and I was the big surprise. I changed beside the car, using the headlights to spot all the zippers, bounced into the house and tried to avoid knocking over any of the emergency candles, or setting my fur on fire as Mom led Bunny up the stairs. When Bunny reached the party he got a bigger surprise than the blackout. These were grade eleven students. From my high school. I made jokes about the school, the teachers and—my big mistake—I called one of the kids by name. That's when I realized I was in trouble. Everybody wanted to know who was under the mask. "Time to get hopping," said Bunny.

And I made a run for it. Naturally, I was followed.

Bob was waiting in the car and was about to call me by name when

I hushed him. Before Bunny could say anything else I was tackled by a half-dozen sixteen-year-old girls and a couple of sixteen-year-old guys. "Rabbit's getting stewed," I said. Everyone was trying to pull the costume off and I was worried they'd rip it—cheesy or not, the costumes were worth a thousand bucks apiece. That's a lot of carrots.

Bunny played a hunch. I called the names of two of the biggest guys there and begged them to help. I promised I'd reveal my true identity at school the next day. The guys, who assumed I was a friend, helped get everyone else off me as I ran for the car. Dr. Bob was sitting on the hood waiting for me.

"This is Bunny's chauffeur," I shouted. "Get in the car and drive, chauffeur." Bob jumped into the driver's seat and Bunny squeezed into the passenger's seat—even though there was no way to close the door. Two of the guys tried to block the car, so Bob wasn't driving until I shouted, "Mow 'em down!" Bob gunned the motor and they dove out of the way. Bob drove a few blocks in the blackout before we realized we didn't have our headlights on. We were almost disappointed the cops hadn't stopped us. It would have been worth it just to see how they wrote us up.

I just realized I don't think I ever kept my promise and told those guys my true identity. I admit it now. It was me.

It was a cool job—but it wasn't going to fund the greatest rock and roll magic show of all time.

12

Pretty Woman

Backstage. Jane wanted to meet us backstage. At the Orpheum. This was serious. This required wearing a shirt with actual buttons.

I couldn't imagine a more glamorous place to meet. The Orpheum was where big concerts happened and the symphony symphed. It was an old vaudeville palace that had just been completely renovated with red plush carpets, posh seats and fancy fixtures—and our promoter wanted us to go to the backstage entrance. And that's where Randy and Kyle and I met the security guard who told us to leave.

"We're here to see Jane," Randy said, "from Rainbow."

"Tickets are on sale at the front," said the security creature.

"We're with the band," said Kyle.

This time the gorilla grunted something.

Kyle grunted back, clearly understanding the guard's pre-verbal communication.

"Stage door," said the guard.

The three of us went to the stage door and mentioned Jane to a slightly more articulate bouncer who said, "Jane's backstage" and handed us three laminated passes to wear like necklaces, then waved us through.

As soon as we stepped inside, the three of us wanted to see, touch and steal. The theatre had the newest equipment in town—the lights, sound system, control boards. "I wanna perform here," said Randy.

So did I. We were definitely not in Kansas, or the Jewish Community Centre, anymore.

Now that we'd officially made it past the gatekeepers no one seemed the least bit interested in us. Spotlights flicked on and off, platforms were being positioned and audio levels set as we made our way to the steps beside the stage. "C'mon up, guys." Jane was on the stage floor, dressed in even shinier, tighter clothes than usual. I think she was wearing leather pants. She looked like a rock star, like Pat Benatar.

As I stepped onto the stage, a rough male voice blasted through the darkness. "You! Kid!" Me? I was dead. I knew I was dead. I was being thrown off the stage, probably out of the building.

"Check the levels."

I stared out at the darkness.

"The microphone," growled the voice. "Grab the mic and talk."

So I picked up the mic next to the guitar stand and did what anyone who'd taken high school acting would do on a newly refurbished vaudeville stage—performed what little I could remember of "To Be or Not to Be." I should have done a monologue from *The Black Metal Fantasy*—that might have been a good omen—but Adoma didn't have a monologue in *Black Metal Fantasy*.

Santar had lots of monologues, but when I handed Kyle the mic naturally he belted out a verse of *Born to Run*. As Kyle did Bruuuuuuuuuce I stood and stared at those seats, imagining our standing ovation until a roadie rolled out the drum kit and broke the spell.

Then Jane led us into the wings. While we were still reeling from the idea of playing three-thousand-seat theatres, we heard a soft southern drawl say, "Hello, Janey, dear." We turned to see an old man in fifties sunglasses—and Johnny Cash-style country singer clothes.

He was wearing so much pancake makeup he might have been embalmed. "How's it going?"

I knew the guy was important. I turned to Kyle and whispered, "Who's that?"

Kyle didn't even look at me as he whispered back, awestruck, "Roy Orbison." Kyle kept staring at Orbison, probably hearing Roy's hits in his head. He didn't just know and love classic rock, he might have been the only teenager in the world who owned blues albums. I figured I'd better not tell Kyle—or Jane—that what impressed me most was that I'd thought Roy Orbison died in that plane crash with Buddy Holly. As Kyle looked into Roy Orbison's sunglasses he saw a perfect reflection of Charlie's golden ticket to the Chocolate Factory. We all did.

I watched Jane flash her smile at the rock legend. "Good house tonight, Roy." She called him Roy. He called her Jane. Sure Jane wasn't old enough to have bought one of his albums back when they were topping the charts, but still … our promoter was talking to a real star just before his concert. Backstage. I felt like asking for an autograph on principle.

"Need anything, Roy?"

"I'm good," said Roy. Then he smiled at her—and us—and moseyed on.

"Have a great show tonight," said Jane. I suspected she didn't say "Break a leg" because he looked old enough that if he did, he'd break a hip too and never recover, but still …

Right after Roy went onstage for his sound check, Cousin Jane handed us the contract. "Here it is," she said. "Your future."

And Roy started singing *Pretty Woman*.

I turned to Kyle. "Why's he singing a Linda Ronstadt song?"

Kyle gave me the look of complete and utter scorn I'd braced for when he'd found out I was a virgin. "It's his song."

"I think he has a higher voice than Linda's."

Kyle scowled.

"And I bet she wears less makeup, too," I said.

Kyle laughed.

"One day," Jane said, "you guys are gonna be out there." And we looked back out at the endless rows of plush seats. We'd already pictured them filled with fans cheering for us, but this wasn't just our fantasy any more. Jane was a real promoter, she worked with real stars, and she was telling us this was going to happen. We watched Roy finish his song, fondled our backstage passes and thought—one day that's gonna be us. Then Randy pulled a deck out of his pocket and asked Jane to pick a card ...

As we walked out through the stage door we practically floated by the security creature and the three of us waved at him like we were old friends.

After Randy and I got back to the apartment, we sat on my bed and watched *The Tonight Show* while Randy absently made a coin dance between his fingers. Paul Lynde, the centre square from *Hollywood Squares*, was on the couch being interviewed.

"That's gonna be us, ya know."

It took me a moment to register what he was talking about. "On *The Tonight Show*?"

"Yeah," said Randy. "And he'll be asking us all about *The Black Metal Fantasy*."

And for a moment I could see exactly what Randy was seeing. Johnny—he'd let us call him Johnny—would have Randy, Kyle and me on as his guests, the star guests who came out right after the monologue and his wacky sketches.

We'd laugh about how this had all started with a handful of store-bought magic tricks on a tacky Community Centre stage that always smelled of stale varnish. We'd tell Johnny how this show was only the beginning. If he thought part one was exciting, wait until the world saw part two and then—the final, ultimate, epic conclusion—part three, *The Battle of the Sorcerors*.

Johnny would laugh, and tell the world what "brilliant kids" we were—he called everybody under forty "kids." Then he'd bring out the band. Our band. Now that we were touring the world, playing New York, London, Tokyo and whatever the biggest city in Australia was, our band would be Styx, Led Zeppelin or maybe Pink Floyd.

Our band would play one of the songs I'd written lyrics for—something with lots of power chords, a supernatural synthesizer riff, and the crowd would go wild, singing along to the number one tune on the *Billboard* charts.

We all need fantasy.
Fantasy keeps us aliiiiiive.
It can get so cold in reality.
Without our dreams how could we ever survive.
Without our dreams how could we ever surviiiiiive.

During the commercial break, before he brought out the guy with the emu, the gibbon and the creepy baby lizard, Johnny would tell us how much he'd enjoyed the Broadway production and invite us back to a party at the Playboy Mansion to frolic with half-naked Bunnies. Since we were all from Vancouver, we didn't realize the Mansion was in Chicago and Johnny was in LA. And even if we had known more about US geography, if anyone had a private jet, Johnny did.

Maybe *The Black Metal Fantasy* wouldn't get quite that big that fast—maybe we'd never sip pina coladas in the grotto with Hef and his pneumatic squeeze, Barbi Benton—but it could. The biggest concert promoter in the country told us it could.

We weren't just crazy teenagers any more. Rainbow was going to make us stars.

13

Signing in Blood

I told Sarah the news while we were walking home from school, a few weeks before grad.

"That's great," she said. And she looked impressed.

"I have something to tell you, too."

She did? She had something to tell me? This was great. There was only one thing it could be. She'd come to her senses, realized Chad or Steve or Frank or Gurk of the Gorilla clan wasn't worthy of her. She loved me and wanted me to be her grad date. I was so busy coming up with what I wanted her to say that I had to ask her to repeat the words she'd spoken.

"Isn't that amazing?

"Amazing," I said, feeling pretty much the same as I had just before I threw up on her on the Ferris wheel. Then she hugged me. She'd never hugged me before. But I didn't feel her body, just its absence. She was going away for the summer, then going away to school. In California. She was going away. I could become a star and she'd never even notice. I couldn't tell anybody else about this, so that night I went over to Bob's house and told him.

"That's great," he said.

"Great?"

"She just wants to be friends. She's never going to want to be more than just friends. Trust me."

I really hated Bob. Just because he was two years older than me and had actually dated girls, he thought he knew more about them than I did.

"So I guess that means you're not doing the show."

Of course I was still doing the show. I had to do the show.

"I thought you were getting a summer job."

"This is a summer job."

"Are you getting paid?"

Paid? Even though he was in university, Bob was so naive. "I'm gonna be rich."

He didn't laugh. That's probably why we're still friends. "Are your parents okay with this?"

"I wanna be a writer," I said. "This is perfect."

"Yeah. And your mom wants you to be a lawyer."

"She doesn't want me to be a lawyer."

"Right, she just wants you to go to law school. She tells everyone you're going to Dalhousie to study law."

"You worry too much," I said. Then I started mooning over Sarah again, wondering how long it would be before *The Black Metal Fantasy* tour hit California ...

The contract with Rainbow was longer than the script for the show. Actually, it was only three pages, but it felt longer and it used bigger words—which was impressive since I'd used every big word I could think of, even if my script was completely lacking in heretofores and whereases. Randy didn't look at the paper; his eyes were fixed on Jane. He loved the idea that she was in our apartment, on our couch. He'd even cleaned the place, made his bed and tossed out the garbage for the first time since moving in. As soon as she sat down he made a string of shiny silk scarves appear.

Jane laughed, applauded and told us the contract was "standard."

"We'll sign in blood," said Randy. He was already reaching for a pen when I suggested that maybe we shouldn't be signing at all. I wasn't good at math but, "30 percent of everything we ever make seems like a lot."

"We take a lot," said Jane. "But we do a lot, too. We do all the PR and marketing, we'll line up the tour, find the venues, handle all the media. We make you stars."

"And then you'll sleep with me, right?" Randy flashed his most charming grin.

Jane smiled back, but from where I was sitting it looked like the answer was no.

"I trust you," he said.

But before Randy could sign the papers, Kyle grabbed them. "Maybe we should have a lawyer look at these."

Lawyer? We didn't have a lawyer.

Randy reached to get the papers back. "If it's standard ..." Randy looked at Jane to see if she was insulted by our lack of faith. She wasn't.

"You should show it to your lawyer," said Jane.

"How much do you give us to do the show?" Kyle asked.

For the first time since we met her, cousin Jane looked surprised. "What do you mean?"

"You're the producer," said Kyle. "So shouldn't we get the budget first?"

Jane finally managed to spit out the word "money." Then a full sentence: "We don't give you money."

Now it was our turn to freeze. I'd thought "produce" meant "pay for." So had Randy. So had Kyle.

"We're not producers," said Jane, "we're promoters."

But she said they were producing the show. Brad said ...

"We're producing the tour. Not the show. That means we find the venues. And we get people to show up. You can afford this, can't you?" she asked. "If you don't have the money ..."

"No problem," said Randy, like he was Houdini and we'd

challenged him to escape from a wet paper bag. "We have an investor." This was starting to rival "No problem" as Randy's default response to all ... non-problems.

Jane sighed. "Good."

Then he asked Jane if she wanted to see his handcuffs and before she could respond he'd already handed her the pair of silver, metal police-issue specials and asked her to lock him up. "Where are the keys?" she asked.

"I can't remember," he said. "I haven't needed keys for them in years." And it didn't take him long to prove it.

Kyle asked if he could bring the contract home. He did. He showed it to his dad.

Kyle came to our apartment the next day to tell us his dad didn't want him to sign. Randy and I both had the same thought. Kyle had to sign. He was the star. We couldn't do the show without him.

"I'll still do it. I just don't want to produce it. I'm an actor," he said. "If I sign this, I'm a producer. I'm responsible for putting on the show. I'm ..." and the next words were key, "financially responsible."

"But you'll get rich," said Randy.

"You'll still pay me," said Kyle. "I'll still get rich. I just don't want to be a producer. I never wanted to be a producer."

Neither did I. Neither did Randy. The two of us weren't going to pay for this. That's what the investor was for.

"I'll make my deal with you. You make your deal with Rainbow." We all agreed that when we made money, we'd share it.

"No problem," Randy said.

"Cool," I said.

"Let's put on a show," Kyle said.

When Kyle left, I felt like leaving with him, but I was already sitting on my bed. I didn't want to produce either. I just wanted to write and direct. And I felt like he'd figured out something I hadn't. The contract scared me, too. It wasn't the specific details, just the idea of signing a contract. It felt legal, grown-up, dangerous. And I'd already moved out of my house to move in with Randy. My dream wasn't as elaborate as his. He'd already designed a mansion based on Hef's—complete with its own grotto, revolving waterbed and nest of Bunnies. I'd just started picturing a life where I could skip university and go directly to fame, fortune and a hotel with a swimming pool.

Randy was happy to produce. He liked the sound of "producer." It was a three-syllable word for "boss." "Let's sign," said Randy.

"Maybe we should show it to a lawyer."

"We can't afford a lawyer," said Randy. "Besides, Jane says it's all standard."

"What about our investor?" I asked. "Can't he hire a lawyer for us?"

"I'll ask," he said.

That night Randy and I watched TV while I tested knots to tie him up and he escaped. After an hour or so he tied my wrists together and taught me the correct way to clench my fists and twist them so if anyone ever did try to trap me I could be out of the ropes inside sixty seconds. We joked about including a rope escape in the show, but agreed that ropes were too tame for Santar.

The next day Randy told me the investor's money was still tied up tighter than either he or I had been the night before, but we'd have all we needed soon. So we still couldn't afford a lawyer, but Randy's mom, Ruth, knew someone. The way Randy talked about her it seemed like Ruth knew everyone. She was a bookkeeper, but she seemed to be friends with celebrities, politicians, my family, everyone else's family and I always got the impression she'd pulled thorns out of a lot of paws, because they all seemed to owe her a favour. At Ruth's insistence, Randy and I put on suits so we went off to discuss our deal for a kick-ass rock musical about demon dimensions looking like we were going to a bar mitzvah.

The lawyer's office was downtown in an art deco building, across from the park where drunks hung out to get drunker. This didn't feel like lawyer-land. But when we walked into the lobby we not only found our lawyer's name on the board, we found "Rainbow." Our lawyer was in the same building as Rainbow. This was a great omen.

When we got to the lawyer's waiting room, it was like somebody'd transported it from another, much more serious building. Ruth was right. This was a place you wore a suit. There were no cool magazines to read, no fishbowls or flowers, just chairs and tables and a cranky receptionist who scowled at us like she was personally offended by the fact that our visit wouldn't be racking up billable hours. She was maybe twenty-five, but looked like she already had the soul of someone who regretted all her life choices. Randy pulled a quarter from her ear anyway because, well, he was Randy. He couldn't even get her to smile. When he made one of her pens disappear, I worried she might bludgeon him with her stapler.

Fortunately, Ruth's friend Sheldon stepped out of his office and called us in before push came to staples. Sheldon checked out our suits, shook our hands and offered us seats. It all felt very formal until he turned to Randy and grinned. "So Ruth says you boys are doing a little magic show. I love magic."

"And rock and roll," said Randy proudly.

Sheldon nodded again. "That's great. I've done a lot of work with rockers." He waved to show us all the gold and platinum records on his walls. "From clients," he said.

I'd never seen a gold record in real life and never heard of a platinum one. This guy was obviously major. I put the contract on his desk. "We were just wondering about this."

Sheldon looked at it and his smile vanished.

"Is it that bad?" asked Randy.

"It's with Rainbow," said Sheldon. "Ruth didn't say it was with Rainbow."

"How cool is that?" said Randy.

"Do you know where their office is?" Sheldon asked. He didn't wait for an answer. "Two floors up. I'm their lawyer."

"That's great," Randy and I said in unison.

Sheldon looked at us like we were, well, bar mitzvah boys. "It means I can't advise you."

"But you have to," said Randy.

"I can't," he said. "I work for Rainbow. They're one of my biggest clients. It's a conflict of interest."

But if he knew all about them wasn't he the best lawyer in the world for us? "Can't you just tell us if it's fair?" asked Randy. "Please?"

"You have to get another lawyer."

Randy didn't quite beg, but it was close enough. "Can't you tell us anything?"

Sheldon stared out the window at the park full of drunks, then looked at the paper and back at us. "I can't comment on the contract. But I can tell you what you should do before you sign a contract like this. You have to incorporate."

"Why?" I asked.

"Liability," he said. We both stared at him blankly. "That way if anyone sues, they're suing the company, not you. Also, it establishes the business and the partnership. Your mom said you were going to be partners, is that right?"

Randy nodded.

Incorporation. It sounded like a magic trick.

"I can incorporate you. I can do that." Then Sheldon stared at me like he was trying to figure out where he knew me from, but that wasn't it. "Are you nineteen? You have to be nineteen to sign a contract or it's not legal."

I didn't say anything. There was no way I was going to screw this up just because of a stupid thing like my birthday.

"You know, if it's only for one show, you should probably just do a partnership agreement."

"We're gonna be rich," said Randy.

I agreed. "We're going to do lots of shows."

"It's part of a trilogy," said Randy.

"Great," said Sheldon. "If there's a lot of money involved, you really have to incorporate."

Back on the street I told Randy that if we were going to be partners, I needed to know about our mysterious investor. Now.

After telling me again that it was a secret, he offered up the name. And I couldn't believe it. Norman? Seriously? Norman? "I don't think I've ever even seen Norman buy his own cigarettes. Isn't he always mooching from you and Kyle?"

"He got an inheritance," said Randy. "A big inheritance."

"That's great," I said. "So why's it a secret?"

Randy's head swivelled and I saw he'd been distracted by a couple of women on the other side of the street. They were both wearing halters and very short shorts. "I love summer," he said. One of them flashed Randy a smile before he continued. "People are weird about money."

I got that. "We really should do a budget. Let Norman know how much we need."

"No problem," he said. "I'll meet up with Norman, see how much it'll cost to build all the tricks."

Four hundred dollars later—two hundred from Randy's paycheque and two hundred from my bunny money—Sheldon waved his magic lawyer stamp and, presto, Black Metal Fantasy Productions was born.

Randy was president.

I was secretary, because every company needed one—although I also took the title "creative director" because it sounded cooler than vice-president.

Kyle didn't want to be part of the company. "I'm just an actor," he said.

"But we're a team," said Randy.

"If you want to you can get me a business card that says *star*."

I suspected Kyle might have been more enthusiastic about being an official part of the company if we hadn't invited him to pay one third of the incorporation costs. By the time Randy and I had opened the bank account, ordered the cheques, bought a corporate seal and printed the business cards—featuring a set of spooky demonic eyes Kyle drew for us—we were out just over six hundred dollars.

Now it was time to sign the contract with Rainbow—the contract our lawyer couldn't comment on, the one that guaranteed our new promoters/partners 30 percent of everything we ever made at the box office. Forever.

"This is great," said Randy. "It's historic."

"I dunno," I said.

"Rainbow's huge," he said. "They're the best." As Randy picked up the black metal pen we'd agreed to sign with we noticed there was only space for one signature on behalf of Black Metal Fantasy Productions and that's when I had an idea. Actually, it was less of an idea than an impulse. "Don't sign it."

Randy looked like I slapped him.

"Just let me sign it," I said.

"You can't," said Randy. "I'm the president."

I pointed at the signature line. "All it says is, 'On behalf of Black Metal Fantasy Productions,' it doesn't say president."

"But you're only seventeen. You're not supposed to sign anything."

"Right," I said. "If you sign it, it's legal. If I sign it, and if anything goes wrong ..."

Randy looked like I'd insulted his honour. "Why would anything go wrong?"

"Exactly. If nothing goes wrong, they'll never know I was too young to make the deal. But if it does ..."

"What do you think's gonna go wrong?"

"Nothing," I said. I tried to think of an example. I couldn't. But I also couldn't shake the feeling that Kyle didn't want to be part of this for a reason.

Randy wasn't convinced. "Doesn't that make you the boss? I mean if you sign it, it's like it's your deal." I realized his problem had nothing to do with ethics.

"It's still your show," I said.

"You're sure?"

"You're the magician," I said.

"But we don't wanna get Jane mad."

"You heard what Sheldon said. This isn't a deal with Jane. It's a deal with Rainbow."

Randy held his pen over the signature line, stared at it, stared at me.

"I'm still the president, right?"

"Definitely," I said. "I'm only seventeen. Legally, I don't even exist."

14

Prophet Participation

The last words I typed when I finished the script were "The beginning of an epic." There was no way I was writing "The end." Then I went back to the front page and drew a little copyright symbol on it, to make sure no one would even think of stealing our story, especially that sneaky Andrew Lloyd Webber. Then I waited for Randy to get home to read it.

I hadn't figured out a way to fit Oryon into the story yet, but we needed a narrator to set up our mystic universe. So Randy would be the narrator—opening and closing the night with major illusions. That way it would still feel like his show.

Our first scene was modelled after *Star Wars*, of course. Instead of the scrolling "long time ago in a galaxy far, far away," Randy would walk out and welcome our audience. "Just make sure you give me a lot of cool lines," he said. So I'd written plenty of narration ....

"Greetings mortals, I am here to welcome you. You have now passed through the portals of your reality and entered into the realm of fantasy. The journey has taken you beyond the boundaries of knowledge and familiarity into a mystical domain where all is possible, as it is governed by the unexplained, the cosmic paradox ... magic."

Any words Stan Lee might write into a *Thor* comic, or Stevie Nicks would use in a song lyric, were welcome here.

Tathania was our wicked witch. Gamatria was our good witch. Or, as Tathania said to Gamatria, "Your heart is soft ... for a demon." Both women had been driven away from their homes as children by superstitious peasants who were going kill them because of their powers or, if you're an *X-Men* fan like I was, their mutant gifts. Think Scarlet Witch and Quicksilver. I did.

Our sorceress sisters were "rescued" by the demon lord, Santar (Magneto). Santar saw himself as Satan's rival and had dreams of conquering hell—as soon as he took down Oryon, the pesky protector of Medemptia. Santar had made a deal with Satan to exchange his chosen disciple for more power, but revealed in one of his numerous soliloquies that if Gamatria was able to survive "the trials," she had enough raw power to help him defeat Oryon and Satan. Our victim—the guy we were going to kill—would be chosen by Gamatria and summoned by her powerful magicks.

What else could I call it but, *The Initiation*? We had appearances, disappearances, levitations, escapes, a sword going through our victim's body and as many flash pots as we could fit onto the stage. We had everything. There was nothing funny in the script.

Nothing intentionally funny anyway—except my stage directions. After Gamatria snapped out of her trance I wrote, "She performs a ritual involving Mazola and a can of spray paint." I might not have had sex yet, but now that I lived with Randy I'd read *Penthouse*. Before the appearance of Satan I wrote, "The music starts and Randy proves why he's president of this outfit." Randy loved that one. After the appearance of Satan I wrote, "If you smell brimstone, run!"

I wasn't sure it worked so I showed the script to anyone who was willing to read it. Randy loved it. Kyle loved it. Jane loved it. Bob thought it was ... okay. Randy showed it to his mother, Ruth, who showed it to a famous local actor. Ruth reported back that the script was a hit. "He said it was brilliant." I was thrilled.

I gave it to my playwriting and directing teacher, Mr. Denos, who said it was, "very well written" and "structured like a Greek tragedy." Apparently I'd managed to absorb all the tragic basics from the old masters at DC and Marvel.

We had a script. Each illusion had its own set-up—a challenge by Santar, or a battle, or a ritual—and its own song. It was going to be a true rock and roll fantasy.

Our battle with paperwork was scarier than anything in the script. Randy and I sat at the kitchen table until 4 a.m. to review the budget. The best we could come up with was that if we got really lucky we could pull this off for just under ...

"Thirty thousand dollars," said Randy. I'd never imagined spending that much money on anything except, maybe, a house. Did a house even cost that much? But the budget looked like it made sense. Randy figured each major illusion would cost at least two thousand dollars. I'd called recording studios to get estimates on how much it would cost to record a soundtrack. And then we'd have to pay everybody. "Thank God Rainbow's promoting us," said Randy.

"Definitely," I said. At least we wouldn't have to worry about marketing, or theatre rental or ticket sales. Our promoter would handle that. "You think Norman can afford this?" I asked.

"No problem," said Randy, and he invited Norman over to talk to us that night. When Norman arrived, Randy never even got the chance to show him the budget.

"I've got something to tell you," said Norman.

By the time Norman finished talking, we could hardly breathe. In the sitcom *Sanford and Son*, every time the son did something that upset the dad, Dad would clutch his heart and shout, "This is the big one. I'm coming to join you, Elizabeth!" If Randy had been a few years older this definitely would have been the big one. Norman didn't have thirty thousand. He didn't have twenty thousand. He didn't even have enough money to pay Randy for the smokes he'd been mooching. What was staggering was that Norman didn't have an explanation either, except that his parents had told him he probably shouldn't touch his inheritance until he was twenty-one. Not even can't. Shouldn't. "I did set you up with Jane, though," said Norman. "So that's like producing, right?"

Randy couldn't talk. But the look in his eyes made it pretty clear the answer was no. I knew what we could do with Norman. He could be the audience member we'd kill on opening night. Maybe we'd light him on fire. And we wouldn't have to figure out a way for him to survive. The screams would be so authentic. And this was Jane's cousin—what if no Norman meant no Jane? I wanted to go to sleep, wake up and find out that Randy had already opened a Black Metal Fantasy bank account with a million dollars in it.

After a long late-night walk to the beach we decided to look at the numbers again to cut out everything we could think of that we didn't need—like salaries. And instead of hiring designers and buying illusions, we could find a free space and volunteers to build the set ourselves. "Do you know how to build?" he asked.

I should have. Construction was in my blood. My Zayda Ben had started his furniture business by learning to repair stoves, but my brother inherited all those genes. In a grade twelve mechanical aptitude test, I scored so low that my guidance counsellor was convinced I'd tanked the test as a joke. There were twenty pictures of tools. I correctly identified the hammer and the saw. The thing I would have sworn was a screwdriver turned out to be something called an "awl"—which I filed away as a potential Scrabble word and never did bother to learn the purpose of.

So if nobody got paid and we didn't have to rent rehearsal space and we could find a free place to build the sets and props we thought we might, just might, be able to pull it off for fifteen thousand dollars.

We were dead. We needed Norman. Except Norman wasn't real. Our producer was an illusion. "Where are we gonna get fifteen thousand bucks?"

Randy's eyes glazed over like he was stoned, but he wasn't. It was more like he'd gone empty, like he'd read the sign on the entrance to hell and abandoned all hope. "We need a new producer."

Randy was right. We needed a new producer.

"Your family has money." He looked at me, like the money was mine. "Your grandfather's rich." Randy was right again. My family had money, at least some people in it did, but I'd never asked for any. I'd paid for my comics and Slurpees with a paper route, by picking up garbage after school with a stick with a spike poking out of it (the vice-principal paid me five dollars an hour), and by dressing up in funny animal costumes.

My Zayda Ben had offered to buy me a car when I turned sixteen. I turned him down. My dad had loaned me his old Honda Civic instead and I'd been saving up to buy it from him no matter how many propeller beanies I had to wear to get it. Zayda Ben was always happy to help people out, but once when the two of us were out for lunch at White Spot he told me he wondered if people would still love him if they didn't need something from him. I was sure he was being sarcastic, frustrated at some request that had hit him at the wrong time on a bad day, but I never wanted him to wonder that about me. That day I promised myself I'd never ask him for anything more expensive than a mushroom burger platter. Yes, people are weird about money.

I couldn't go to my parents either. Not only would they not give me the money, they might have me committed. Besides, I didn't want a loan, or a gift. I wanted an investor. I wanted someone who believed ...

Then I thought of my Uncle Stanley. He was my mom's youngest brother and he worked for my grandfather. Even though he was only ten years older than me—or maybe because he was only ten years older than me—we weren't particularly close. But I'd heard him talk about investments and I knew he loved comics—it was his old comics, the ones Grandma hadn't donated to the Children's Hospital that started my collection. So I thought, just maybe ...

It seemed bizarre to arrange a formal meeting with my uncle. But I wanted this to be official. Randy and I both did.

We arranged to meet at Stanley's office. I told him I wanted to talk about the show. He knew a bit about it. Everyone in my family knew I'd written a magic show that was being produced by Rainbow. Randy wore his suit. I couldn't bring myself to wear a suit to see my uncle—that seemed too weird—but I wore proper slacks and a shirt with buttons instead of my standard T-shirt.

Uncle Stanley decided that if we were going to pretend to be business people, he'd go along with the game. "So what can I do for you two gentlemen?" he asked.

Randy had prepared a speech and rehearsed it for me. It included phrases like "investment opportunity." But this was my uncle. Before Randy could say much more than "Rainbow Productions," I blurted out the truth: "We're in trouble." We told him everything. We told him about Norman. And how we'd thought Rainbow producing meant Rainbow was paying, not just taking 30 percent.

And we told him how this would be the biggest magic show ever, but we had no idea how to pay for it and needed fifteen thousand dollars now, or we'd have to cancel. He listened, nodded a lot, grunted politely and, when we finished, leaned back in his chair and studied our faces.

Randy looked desperate. I don't know how I looked, but I know how I felt—humiliated that I'd asked someone, anyone, for money, and I wanted to take all the words back and burn them. I also knew that if Uncle Stanley didn't believe in us that *The Black Metal Fantasy* was over. I was seventeen years old, days away from graduating and I was going to spend the rest of my life regretting how I'd made a once-in-a-lifetime shot at superstardom disappear because of fifteen thousand—

"I like the name," he said. "*Black Metal Fantasy*. Like the *Heavy Metal* comics."

"I love *Heavy Metal* comics," said Randy. "Aren't they the coolest thing ever?"

"Pretty much," said Stanley. "Pretty much."

Did this mean ...

"I can't loan you fifteen thousand dollars," he said.

I knew it. "That's okay," I said, wishing Randy could make me vanish.

"I think we can do ten," he said. And he smiled.

This couldn't be happening. There's no way he just said ...

"It's a loan though, not an investment. I'll want it back. With a share of the profits. So we'll have to work a deal out on profit participation here."

I could have cried, but I was too shocked. So was Randy. It couldn't be this easy. I was too startled to say a word. Finally, I mustered an "Are you sure?"

Randy looked ready to kill me, but I had to ask. This wasn't Norman, this was family.

Stanley leaned forward in his chair to examine us both before looking me straight in the eyes. "Is it gonna be a good show?"

Of course it was. It was gonna be the best show ever. And we had ten thousand dollars to make it work.

"It's gonna be huge," I said.

While Randy stumbled over a "Thank you," Stanley took out his chequebook. "Who do I make it out to?"

I said it first: "Black Metal Fantasy Productions Limited."

But this wasn't a fantasy anymore. We had the money to put on a show.

And Randy found his poise, enough poise for both of us, and said what we were both thinking: "You're gonna be rich. We're all gonna be rich."

Just before he handed over the cheque, Stanley asked one more question. "Rainbow is really producing this?"

"Their third-ever stage show: *Beatlemania*, *A Chorus Line* and *The Initiation*."

"That's pretty good company," said Stanley as he passed me the cheque. "Don't spend it all in one place." Then, "How's your mom?"

We had a new investor.

When we met Jane to hand off the contract, just as I was about to pass it to her, I asked her what we'd been afraid to ask. "Have you talked to Norman lately?"

She looked at us blankly.

"Your cousin," said Randy.

"He's not working on the show anymore," I said.

"He was working on the show?"

"Yeah," said Randy. "And he was gonna invest his inheritance."

"What inheritance?" asked Jane. "All his relatives are alive."

We had to light him on fire.

Troubled Teens

Dez Fiddler was a real playwright. He'd written *Angst*, which I knew was huge. And he ran Vancouver's major youth theatre company, Canadian Kidz—a company that had just finished a world tour with a rock musical about troubled teens (the only kind of teens adults ever wanted to see on stage). Kyle had taken a class with him and the man himself had offered to give us a bit of advice on producing a show. "Maybe he'll have some useful tips," said Kyle.

I was impressed. "You know Dez Fiddler?" I loved the idea of getting advice from someone who had produced and toured real plays.

More importantly, they'd toured shows to our high school. If anyone was going to be able to tell us how to do this right, it would be Dez Fiddler. So I couldn't believe it when he agreed to meet with us. I jumped around our living room like we'd been offered an audience with the queen. Or Queen. Or Stevie Nicks.

I didn't know what I expected, but when we pulled up in front of Dez Fiddler's office, Randy and I both wanted to turn around. It was almost next to the armory and I parked right in front of a decommissioned tank. This place made our lawyer's seedy building look palatial.

"What a dive," said Randy.

I kept checking the address to see if I'd mixed up the numbers. This didn't look like the headquarters of a world-famous theatre company. It was a seedy storefront office, in a seedy building, in a seedy part of town. Years later I'd discover that's exactly what the headquarters of most world-famous theatre companies looked like.

There was a waiting room with a few stacks of plays, brochures and official-looking forms and, at the back, the office of the man himself. We looked around for the bustling staff, the receptionist, the real office ...

"Come on in," he said. "You must be Kyle's friends."

We introduced ourselves as we carefully cleared old scripts off two chairs that appeared to be leftover props from an ancient high school production.

"I'm Dez," said Dez. He was wearing khaki pants, a flannel work shirt and the gold wire-framed glasses that everybody remotely artsy (including me) wore. He did not look rich or famous. He was supposed to look rich and famous. Randy and I stared at him like we were Hobbits and he was Gandalf. "So," he said, examining us like we weren't what he was expecting either, "I hear you're thinking of producing a show."

I looked to Randy to say something. He didn't, so I had to. "We *are* producing a show."

"Don't do it. Kyle says you don't have any grants."

Grants?

"Do you have any grants?"

I shook my head and resisted asking what a grant was.

"Have you applied for any?"

Applied? To whom? For what? How? Mercifully, Fiddler continued before I could ask any of my questions.

"Then don't do it," repeated Fiddler.

Instead of advice it felt like we'd found ourselves summoned to the vice-principal's office. Or the helpful guidance counsellor who'd told me writing wasn't a real career. "But we've done a budget. We've got ten thousand dollars."

"If you've budgeted ten, it'll cost you twenty. If you're lucky," he said. "Shows always cost twice as much as you think they will."

"Then how do they make money?" Randy said, challenging him.

"Nobody makes money off theatre," said Fiddler.

Randy looked ready to run him through with a sword.

I wasn't going to take this either. "*Angst* made money, right?"

"*Angst* was funded by grants. That was how we paid for the tour. Do you know how expensive it is to take a show on the road? Especially with a band." No wonder this schmuck had lost money, he hadn't talked to Jane. She'd warned us not to travel with a band.

Then Dez told us he'd produced dozens of shows and once he'd paid operating costs and actors and venue rentals and travel, none of them made money either. Most of them lost money. "If it weren't for grants and donations, there wouldn't be a Canadian Kidz Theatre." Randy and I looked at each other knowingly. Maybe this guy could write and direct, but he was obviously a lousy producer.

"And you really don't want to do this in the summer. It's too risky in Vancouver."

"You're doing a show this summer," I said. I'd read about it. He was doing a new musical about troubled street kids.

"But I'm not paying for it," he said. "The federal government is. It's funded by a work-study program for street kids."

"What's wrong with summer?" asked Randy. "Everybody loves to go to movies in the summer."

"But they don't go to live theatre," said Fiddler. "Not in Vancouver. Not if it's sunny. No matter how good the show is, if it's sunny no one goes anywhere except the beach. So unless you can figure out a way to do your show on the beach ..."

Neither of us said it, but we were both thinking it—maybe they don't go to *your* shows Mr. Dez I-fund-my-plays-with-government-money Fiddler, but they'll sure as hell go to ours, because we're doing a show that everybody will want to see.

"If there's anything I can do to help you," he said. "If you don't want to put on the show right away, if you want to look at next year, there are grants you can apply for. I can give you the forms, help you out with them, I can tell you who to call."

"That's okay," said Randy.

It was obvious to both of us what was going on here. Maybe nobody wanted to see his lame shows, but they'd line up to see ours. Our show would have magic and music and Lisa Jorgensen in skimpy costumes.

"I'm not trying to be a downer," he said. "But I'd hate to see you kids lose your shirts."

"Thanks," I said.

"Yeah," said Randy. Then we talked about *Angst* for a few minutes, because we knew it would have been rude to tell him what we were thinking. But Randy said it as soon as the wooden door to his cheap office creaked shut behind us: "What a bitter old guy."

"Yeah," I said.

Randy shook his head, disgusted. "He's gotta be at least thirty."

"At least," I agreed. "Just because he can't make it in theatre, doesn't mean we can't. Let's send him tickets to opening night."

"Sure," said Randy. "If we're not totally sold out."

16

The Necoronomicon

We'd been so worried about how to pay for producing the show that we'd almost forgotten we had to produce the show. If you've ever wondered why most movies are terrible, it's because when you're chasing money, deciphering contracts and juggling egos, there isn't much time left over to deal with trivial details like, you know, making a movie.

We called Lisa in to read the script with us. Randy was dying to show her our place, to show her he was no longer the boy next door.

"It's nice," she said when she stepped inside, which was about the nicest thing anyone could say about the place. Then she said, "I have something to tell you."

When someone says they have something to tell you, it's almost always something you don't want to hear—usually something you really don't want to hear. And Lisa said it in the type of serious tone Randy had only heard once before from a girl—when her period was late. That turned out to be a false alarm. Lisa's news was real. She'd been offered a summer job at a clothing store with a perky name like "Young Ms." The loss of our leading lady was bad enough, but the real crisis was that Randy's fantasies of seducing Lisa on the road were shattered.

"But I thought you wanted to be an actress."

"I'll get free clothes," said Lisa.

"This show could make you rich. And famous. And ..."

"My parents won't let me tour, anyway."

"We'll stay in hotels," he said trying to help her realize how much better this could possibly be than folding T-shirts, or first-year university. Even though Randy was nineteen, he'd never travelled anywhere outside the province except Disneyland. It didn't matter what hotels we were going to stay in, it was the idea of hotels that appealed to him. "They'll have pools and mini-bars and movies on TV."

"You'll find someone else," said Lisa. "You guys'll be great."

Randy didn't know what to say, what to do. He couldn't believe this was happening. *The Black Metal Fantasy* had never just been about fame and fortune—it had always been about the chance to make out with Lisa Jorgensen.

We'd lost our leading lady.

The good news was that we found a place to build. When I told Dr. Bob we needed a workshop, he asked if I'd thought about the rafting trip yet. I told him I couldn't think about anything until we had a place to build. That's when he offered his dad's garage—and he offered to help Randy with the set. Then he reminded me the rafting trip was "only a hundred bucks."

I handed him a cheque.

I also asked my brother David whether he had any time to help build a set. Even though he was only fourteen, I was sure David knew what an awl was. So we had at least a couple of volunteer builders. Now we just needed actors.

While Randy was in shock over Lisa's departure, Kyle and I realized this was the chance to bring in someone new as our leading lady—someone with experience. Maybe someone over seventeen? Kyle and I did up an audition ad. We paid to run it in a community newspaper and sent copies to every high school in the city to the attention of all the grade twelve drama teachers. We rented an answering machine so people could book audition times. I'd never seen an answering machine before. It was about the size of the *Yellow Pages* and held two full-sized cassette tapes—one for the outgoing message, one for incoming calls. It was the newest, coolest thing in the apartment. Buying one cost over three hundred dollars, so we leased ours for twenty-four bucks a month—which seemed like a smart move since we only needed it until August, and once the show was over we'd be rich enough to have a secretary and maybe a whole office.

Since the show was inspired by *Heavy Metal*, and we were teen-aged guys, we knew what our new stars were supposed to look like—cousin Jane, but in a chain-mail bikini like Princess Leia's. But it never occurred to me to say so in our audition notices. Having never held auditions before, we assumed all actresses looked like they could be Angels for Charlie. And we didn't mention age because, well, that never occurred to us either.

Since I'd been in the high school drama festival I knew how to spread the word to high school teachers that we were looking for actors. But I didn't know how to write an ad that would convince "real" actors to audition. Even if I'd written a proper ad, I suspect the line about the auditions being held at the JCC would have put off most of the professionals. That was probably just as well since we hadn't worked out any of the professional details like how long we'd be rehearsing, or where and when we'd tour. And we knew we couldn't afford to pay anyone.

Since the only auditions I'd ever been to consisted of Mr. Denos asking us to read from whichever play he wanted to direct, I didn't know the protocol, but Kyle did. Sort of. He drew a pair of spooky eyes that stared out from the top of our audition form and, underneath the menacing glare, we asked for name, phone number; related experience/past performances; additional performance skills (i.e. mime, dance); and "technical experience or interest." We also asked each woman for age, height, weight, hair colour and sex. Much to our disappointment, no one filled in the last space with "yes" or "any time."

I'd never heard of a headshot and not one of the forty-two females who auditioned brought one. Only six had resumés—and all were handwritten. I was still impressed. Even handwritten resumés seemed pretty official to me. Our star only had two non-school shows to his credit and one of those was *The Black Metal Fantasy*. After the forms were filled out, Randy ushered our potential stars into the perfect audition space for a show about demonic magic—a small room filled with toddler toys because it doubled as the Jewish Community Centre's daycare.

I'd read that Woody Allen held auditions where all he asked actors to do was walk across a stage. I'd thought that sounded inhuman, until we held auditions and I realized that if someone doesn't look like the character in your imagination, it's cruel to make them jump through the hoops to chase a role they're never going to get. At least half the women who showed up could have out-acted Meryl Streep and there's no way we would have cast them. Heck, there's no way we would have cast Meryl Streep. We wouldn't even have cast everyone's 1980 teen dream, Lynda "Wonder Woman" Carter, because she was too much older than Kyle. Whenever a non-contender stepped into the room Randy just scrawled "NO" in block letters on the back of his notepad and tried his best not to look bored.

But since Kyle had never been to an audition where he wasn't asked to perform a scene, it never crossed our minds not to let everyone show us what they'd prepared—including the women who looked nothing like our teen dreams, or the girls who either looked, or were, under sixteen—which meant they were too young to tour the world with us.

We needed two women: Gamatria, the innocent, younger sister with untapped mystic powers and Tathania, the older sister who was less powerful, but had already embraced the *Black Metal Fantasy* equivalent of the dark side. It never occurred to us to do the Betty and Veronica thing where we played blonde versus brunette. So the three of us never discussed hair colour—just attitude, presence and, okay, how much our would-be stars looked like they'd stepped out of a *Heavy Metal* comic book. So even though we had more than forty women show up over the two afternoons of auditioning in the JCC daycare, that left us with only about a half-dozen serious contenders for the two parts.

Eva had prepared two pieces: a Shakespeare and a Neil Simon monologue. Then she did a cold reading from the script where she pronounced every word but "Necronomicon" as well as I could. When we had her do a scene with Kyle, she looked at him more than she looked at the pages she was holding. Eva wasn't *Heavy Metal*, but she was sexy in a tough-Italian-chick-who-could-beat-up-any-guy-who-gave-her-grief sort of way and she'd been in the chorus in a production of *Grease* the year before. The big knock against her—she was sixteen and only in grade eleven which meant it would be tough to tour with her.

Ivy was nineteen, 5'8", 135, with jet-black hair and super-exotic eyes. She didn't have a resumé, but on the sheet she listed all sorts of workshops in singing, dancing and speech. She'd even worked as a stagehand once at a real theatre. This was someone with serious credentials. Our big concern was her size. Despite what it said on his resumé, Kyle wasn't much taller than 5'8" and not a whole lot heavier than 135, so when she stood beside him, Ivy looked like she could take him in a fight.

When we asked her to perform the seduction/torture scene with Kyle, she ran a finger slowly down his chest before touching her long index fingernail to his throat. Randy's notes: "Oh my God. Lucky Kyle!"

I agreed. We had a definite contender.

After Ivy left we had another dozen auditions with girls who definitely weren't *Initiation* material and by 4 p.m. Kyle was begging for a smoke break. I wanted a Slurpee.

Then Tabitha walked into the room like she had her own theme music playing. Maybe she did and we just couldn't hear it. I'd guess it was something sultry and dirty, sung by Marianne Faithfull. "I'm here for the auditions," she announced in a rasp that would have worked for a blues singer as she looked right past Kyle and laser-locked on me. No other woman had looked past Kyle at me. I wasn't sure they even noticed me when I was talking. While she was a little short for a *Heavy Metal* heroine, Tabitha had the build. She had long, wavy brown hair and green cat's eyes—perfect for a sorceress. I checked her age. Sixteen. Grade eleven. Damn. "So you're Mark," she said. "I like the script."

Kyle and I exchanged puzzled looks.

"I got here early. Randy let me read his copy. The writer's name is on it."

"Oh," I said. "Um, thanks."

"Nice use of language," she said. "And I'm looking forward to seeing those illusions—especially the cage. Who's doing the music?"

She talked like she already had the part. "Would you like this?" she asked. And I realized she was still standing in front of me holding our audition sheet and her resumé.

"Yeah," I said. "Sure. Yes."

She handed over the script pages, too, the ones for the audition scene.

"You're gonna need that," said Kyle.

She shook her head. "I've already memorized it."

And she had. Aside from a minor stumble on "Necronomicon"—a word nobody had pronounced correctly—Tabitha made it through the monologue like she'd studied it for weeks. It was the first time the lines sounded like they made sense. The one word I wrote on the back of her sheet in big block letters was "HAUNTING."

"Would you like to try a scene?" asked Kyle.

"What would you like me to do?" Tabitha asked me.

"Read this," I said. Tabitha smiled and nodded as I handed her two pages.

Kyle sat in a chair in the centre of the JCC daycare playing our victim. For the first time since she'd walked in, all Tabitha's focus was on Kyle and she performed the seduction-torture scene like he was the only person in the room, maybe the only person in the world. It wasn't sexy, but it was definitely cool. I had no doubt people would buy this woman as someone who would torture you ... and enjoy every second of it. The moment she finished the scene, her eyes left Kyle like he'd vanished and locked back on mine.

"Would you like me to do anything else?" While I was sure it was my imagination, that question sounded a lot more charged than her audition scene.

I had to look away. I scribbled something illegible on the paper. "Thanks," I said.

She didn't move. I looked back up and her eyes were still fixed on me. "You've got my number," she said.

"Thanks," I said again.

"Thank you," she said. "I really like the script. I love Tolkien and Heinlein and Lovecraft and I'm a big fan of magic. When I was in Toronto a few years ago I saw Doug Henning at the Royal Alex. He was amazing."

She'd seen Henning? Live? I was ready to hire her on the spot. I knew she'd be knocking Sarah out of my dreams that night.

After she left I asked Kyle what he thought.

"Not bad," he said. I was thrown by his tone. Then it hit me— maybe he wasn't going to be too keen on the only actress who didn't seem ready to wrestle his girlfriend from him.

"She's seen Henning," said Randy. "That's cool."

"I kinda like her," I said.

"No kidding," said Kyle. Then he flashed me a "one of the guys" grin I'd never seen from him before. "For a second I thought you two were going to ask us to leave the room."

I looked at Kyle, stunned. "You, uh, think she, uh, liked ...?"

"Either that or she really wants to do this show."

Of course. She knew I was the director. No wonder she was flirting with me. It was still cool but ...

"Yeah," I said, returning to the real world where girls were only interested in Kyle or Randy.

Then, just when we were getting ready to call it a day, Annie walked in.

"She's perfect," Randy said. Kyle and I weren't going to argue. We just told him to keep it quiet so she wouldn't realize we'd already fallen in love with her before she'd said a word.

Annie may not have been an evil sorceress, but like Jessica Rabbit, she was drawn that way. Kyle spoke first. Okay, he coughed, then he spoke. "Do you have anything prepared?"

She smiled. We melted. Then, without missing a beat, she broke into a troubled teen monologue about sex and drugs and broken hearts and—"Gamatria." I wrote on my notepad.

"Tathania," wrote Kyle.

She finished her monologue. Her face was covered with fresh tears. Then she flashed a sweet smile at us. "Is that all?"

Each of our note pages for her were already covered with the word "WOW."

We realized we ought to say something. "Maybe—if you wouldn't—if it would be—could you try?" And I handed her the scene.

All the other actresses had orbited Kyle. Annie attacked him. She had the predatory edge of a film noir femme fatale. As Annie prepared Kyle for his role as a sacrifice, she undid his shirt button by button all the way down to his jeans and, for a moment, it didn't look like she was going to stop there until she screamed the last word of the scene, "Die!" loudly enough to make us both jump. We were ready to hire her on the spot. We were ready to kill for her on the spot.

"Thank you," I said.

"Uh huh," said Kyle.

"We'll call you," said Randy.

"And let you know ..." I said.

"Thanks," said Annie. "That was fun!" And she practically skipped out of the room.

"I need her," said Randy.

"I need a cold shower," said Kyle.

"Wow," said I.

We'd found the perfect fantasy girl for *The Black Metal Fantasy*.

That was when Annie's sister, Tina walked in.

Tina was taller than Annie and her face was more angular, edgier. If they were twins she was definitely the evil·one. "I have a lot more experience than Annie," she said. Perfect.

Then she undid a button on her blouse. Oh, how we wanted to love her. But as excited as I was to be staring straight at these impressive, barely covered breasts I couldn't shake the feeling she shouldn't be flashing them while performing a monologue from *Godspell*. I'm sure that might have been a big thrill for a Christian male of a certain age, but it really wasn't working for me or Kyle. Then she did the Gamatria monologue and it was clear she didn't speak Sword and Sorcery. Tina finished, smiled and said, "Should I do the scene now?"

"No, that's okay," I said.

Tina looked like her head was going to start spinning and spewing pea soup.

"Annie got to do a scene." Now she looked like an evil sorceress.

"Right, sorry. Of course," I said as I handed her the script.

After Tina shouted, "Die!" she turned to us like she'd earned an Oscar and asked if she had the job.

"We'll let you know," said Kyle.

"You better make it fast," said Tina. "I'm up for a job as a hostess at the Keg, but I'd rather act this summer."

"I liked her," said Randy.

"Of course you did," said Kyle.

We knew from the moment she walked in that our last auditioner wasn't a contender. Heidi was pretty, but not in an evil sorceress way—more Barbara Gordon than Batgirl. And when she was acting, she seemed shy, like she was afraid of saying the lines too loudly. We didn't take many notes about her, just enough to make it look like we'd been paying attention. So the three of us were surprised to see her waiting in the hall when we walked out of the room. "I was just wondering..."

"We haven't made up our minds yet," said Kyle.

Heidi didn't let him finish. "No, that's not it. I just thought ..." She looked at me. "I'd really like to direct some day. And I think this could be really cool and ... do you need a stage manager? Or assistant director? Or something? I'd just like to help."

A stage manager? Now that Norman was dead to us, that was a great idea.

"Sure," I said.

Heidi almost hugged me, then stopped herself. "I should give you my number. Oh right, you've got my number. On the audition sheet. I'm Heidi. Okay, so call me!" Now she looked excited.

As soon as Randy, Kyle and I grabbed a table at Bud's, Belushi appeared with two bottles of Corona, my dry apple cider, a basket of chips and a bowl of salsa. If we'd had headshots like real directors, we would have shuffled through them, but we didn't, so I fanned our audition sheets on the table like we were using them for a Tarot reading and we set out to choose the women of our dreams.

"Annie's really hot." It was Randy. Again. He'd repeated the words a dozen times on the drive to Bud's. Kyle and I knew we wanted Annie. We all wanted Annie.

The problem was that Randy wanted Tina, too. "They look perfect," said Randy. "And Tina ..."

"She practically stripped at the audition." Kyle said it like this was a bad thing, but Randy perked up like Kyle had joined his side of the argument.

Kyle and I both shot him a look. If Randy noticed our reactions, it didn't slow him down. "Don't you wanna enjoy your summer? Just call them both back. Put 'em in a scene together. Maybe together they'll be great. Try Tina as Tathania, Annie as Gamatria."

"We need a Tathania who can act," said Kyle.

"Ya know, I used to just use friends as my assistants—girls, guys, I didn't care. And I never cared what they wore. And when I did shows at malls or schools, there were always guys who heckled. Always. Then I did this benefit at Oakridge and all these guys were just starting to heckle and Lisa walked onstage in her *Black Metal Fantasy* costume. The heckling stopped. Everyone thinks it's just about misdirection, you know. You get a beautiful woman up there and they're watching her—but it's not—it's so that the guys who don't wanna watch the magic can watch the girl." He sounded positively ... logical. "Besides," he said, "haven't you ever dreamed of doing sisters?"

I hadn't, but now that he'd put the thought in my head ... Nope, still couldn't picture it. Kyle dipped another chip. "Right now I'm just dreaming about doing a play."

"What about Tabitha?" I asked. "She can act. And she's smart. And ..." I stalled for a moment. "Didn't you think she was kind of sexy?"

Kyle smiled. "I know *you* thought she was sexy."

I'm pretty sure I blushed.

"I wouldn't kick her out of bed for eating crackers," said Randy. The crackers concept threw me even more than the sisters thing.

"Great eyes," said Kyle. "Intense. Kinda ..."

"Sexy," I suggested.

"Scary," he said. "She could work."

"Fine," said Randy. "We'll bring back Annie and Tina and Tabitha and ..."

"Ivy and Eva," I said.

"And you should ask Heidi out," said Randy.

"I think Randy's right on this one," said Kyle. "Read the signals."

"What signals?"

"Nobody wants to stage manage," said Kyle.

"Shouldn't we work together first?" I asked.

Both Randy and Kyle looked at me like I'd failed my own audition. "The first time you meet a girl you've gotta set up that you're interested, or it's never gonna go anywhere," said Randy. "That's why I always flirt with every girl I meet, cause you never know."

Cool. So all I had to do to fix things with Sarah was fly around the world like Superman to go back in time and make my move on the swing set in elementary school. "Have you even kissed a girl?"

"Yeah," I said—much too defensively. I was pretty sure he didn't believe me.

"Who?"

Randy had stopped looking at me and was checking out the singer taking the stage—a country and western babe in skin-tight Levi's, leather boots, leather vest and black cowboy hat. Randy grinned. "I should go tell her I can make her a star."

I had kissed a girl, but now I couldn't remember her name. "The representative from France." I was digging myself in deeper. "At the model UN. Kathy. Her name was Kathy."

"Man, you're such a nerd," said Randy. I had to admit it sounded pretty nerdy.

Randy laughed, and said he couldn't stop thinking about Annie and Tina. While he pictured Annie and Tina, I pictured them too, but I suspect with a lot more clothes on. And I pictured Tina killing me in a wild rage when I told her we wanted Annie and didn't want her.

17

Falling Angel

I phoned our contenders to invite them for callbacks. We had to do the callbacks on Sunday because during the week the daycare room was being used for the preschool kids at Jewish day camp and I didn't think little Benji and Reesa and Shlomo were ready to watch a half-dozen sexy girls pretend to seduce Kyle while praising the glories of Satan.

We had each actress try a new monologue as Gamatria and then do the scene where Tathania had to mime being stuck in a shrinking cage—a sort of invisible version of the trash compactor in *Star Wars*. It was our only major non-magical illusion. We were going to do it with a mix of mime, music and killer lighting.

Eva came across as too tough for our conflicted sorceress, Gamatria, but she had potential as Tathania.

Then Ivy took the stage, or at least the area we were using as our stage. Looking at her again, I realized there was something mysterious about her that really worked for our falling angel. I also started thinking her size could work in our favour if I had her play small until the moment she challenged Santar, and then she could stand up straight and we'd get a sense of her full power.

Next up was Tabitha. She still seemed to have her own theme music, but today's tune was louder and raunchier. Once again, she was practically off-book by the time she did the scene. There was something about her—the way she talked, her confidence with the language, her eyes ... And I loved how she said my lines like she knew them. She hissed the angry words, purred the sexy ones, and made the ones I'd written to fill space while tricks were being performed sound like they meant something. I covered her sheet with positive comments. Randy and Kyle didn't write a word.

Then it was Annie's turn. We'd saved the sisters for last, so we could try them as a team. Now that she'd had a day to prepare, and we'd all recovered from our lust at first sight, we realized Annie wasn't perfect—but she was close. If Randy could have built the *Black Metal Fantasy* dream girl in a lab, when he lifted the sheet to shout, "It's alive!" she would have looked like Annie. She seemed vulnerable as Gamatria, savage as Tathania and sexy enough that when we put her picture on the poster—and we had to put her picture on the poster— we'd sell a million tickets.

"I'm still in love," wrote Randy.

We all were.

And then ... Tina.

"It is a pity that only one of us may be ordained." That was a line from the script. Annie was saying it.

Tina squinted at Annie. I think she was trying to sneer. "That it is, but if he chose two, the death of one would be inevable, for to be high priestess is also to be ..."

I had to say something. "Inevitable."

"Sorry," said Tina. "Inevitable ... Who talks like that?"

"It's okay," said Randy. "You were great."

He was lying. He had to be lying. I barely bothered to take notes, but Randy had already written "EXCELLENT TATHANIA" in the centre of his sheet and circled it.

Kyle's nicest note on Tina was, "Much better than I expected."

"So?" asked Tina.

"You were great," Randy said again.

"Hey, I'm planning my summer. I wanna know now."

"We have to see a few more people," I said.

"Bullshit," said Tina.

Annie put a hand on her sister's arm. "Take it easy."

Tina pulled away. "Don't worry, Annie. They know, they're just being assholes. So what's it gonna be? I gotta call the Keg and tell them whether I'm gonna take the hostess job."

That was it. I didn't care what Randy's fantasies were about sisters. I had to say something. "We have to ..."

"Take the job," said Randy.

Kyle and I both turned to look at him. Tina was shocked, but not as shocked as we were. "Fine. C'mon." Tina took her script and tossed it on the ground. Papers scattered everywhere as Annie and Tina started for the door. I stood up and tried to sound like Tina didn't scare me.

"Actually, I kinda wanna talk to Annie."

Tina looked like she was going to spontaneously combust—my ultimate illusion.

"Are you seriously telling me you want Annie and not me?"

Nobody wanted to say it—or maybe we all wanted to say it, but were too afraid she'd kill us. Kyle took over. "Yeah."

Now Tina had gone from violent to wounded and I wasn't sure what was scarier. "I'm trained. I took classes." She was going to cry. We were about to make the scariest woman I'd ever met cry. I felt awful, I felt like ...

"Fuck you!"

Just fine. I felt just fine.

Annie looked at her sister, looked at us. She started to follow Tina, but hesitated just long enough for Tina to blow her last fuse and let loose with another half-dozen nuclear f-bombs before glaring at Annie. "And you can take the bus home!"

Annie ran back into the room grinning like she'd been named Miss America. "You guys really like me?"

"You were great," said Randy.

"You're in," said Kyle.

"Which part?" she asked.

We exchanged puzzled looks. Annie was our first choice for both parts.

"We'll call and let you know," I said.

We had two second choices for Tathania. I was, um, hot for Tabitha. Kyle liked Eva. But they were both sixteen. Randy felt there was no point even discussing second choices. "It has to be Annie." We all agreed

"If only she had a sister," said Randy. Kyle and I glared. But this time he laughed. "Just kidding. So who's Gamatria?"

As much as I wanted Tabitha in the show, as much as I wanted an excuse to see Tabitha again, she had way too much edge to be our innocent sister. I held Ivy's sheet in my hand, smiled at Kyle. "You okay with making out with her?"

"I can cope," said Kyle.

Why hadn't I written a part for Adoma—with a love scene?

But we still had one more day of auditions.

"I guess I should take my shirt off."

They were the words we'd all been dreaming of since we'd first announced our auditions. Unfortunately, these were the auditions for the victim, so it was a tough-looking nineteen-year-old guy doing the talking. Before anyone could respond, he was peeling like this was an audition for *Chippendales*. And there he was, topless, right in front of the Fisher Price play sets, trucks, dollies and hula hoops.

Dougie had heard about the show from Tina. He'd performed with her in *Godspell*. The way he smiled when he said Tina's name made us suspect he'd performed with her offstage, too.

I'd asked Heidi to be our stage manager; I couldn't bring myself to ask her on a date. Besides, she'd directed three plays for her high school. By our standards those were practically professional credits. I wanted her at the auditions for the victim because I knew stage managers were supposed to go everywhere the director went. And since she wanted to direct I figured maybe she'd have some ideas. When Dougie took his shirt off it sure looked like she was getting ideas.

Also, I wanted a third set of eyes because Randy wasn't there. He was shopping for gear to build the illusions. "I don't need to see guys audition," he'd told us.

Dougie's muscles didn't impress me. He had a lot of them, but I wasn't sure if it mattered how strong he was. The main things our victim had to do were plead for his life, panic, scream and die. But it was impossible not to notice that he had one unexpected qualification for the role. He already had a prominent knife scar. When I saw that I scrawled down "I hope he's good."

We had him audition with Ivy, since she was the one who had to kill him. He read about as well as Tina had, and just as I was ready to bring in our next victim, he screamed. It was a shock to discover a guy that tough could scream so well, like he really was afraid of dying. None of the other guys remotely impressed us. They all looked like kids. They all *were* kids. Dougie was nineteen and looked older, like he'd spent time in the real world.

I asked Dougie to forget the script and improvise around the scene. As soon as he was making up his own words—which were shorter and included a lot more swearing—he was completely believable. After Dougie left the room, we started to share our thoughts.

Kyle thought he was cool.

Heidi thought he was hot. "He's not my type. But I'm just saying, you've got these two hot girls walking around in next to nothing for the whole show, do you really think the girls in the audience are gonna be that upset when you rip this guy's shirt off?"

Girls in the audience. I hadn't thought about girls in the audience. I liked Heidi's logic.

Suddenly Kyle looked a bit less enthusiastic. "He wasn't great with the lines."

"He's intense though," said Heidi.

And he had a scar.

Heidi caught Dougie on the way out of the building and brought him back to the room. I asked if he wanted the gig. He gave me a hug that nearly crushed me. After Dougie, Kyle and Ivy left to bond over a smoke, Heidi turned to me and asked if I could give her a ride home. I said, "Sure."

We were almost at her place when I asked her something I'd been wondering for a while. "So if you don't like guys like Dougie, what is your type?"

"I like them with a little more brains," she said. Then she smiled.

18

The Manifesto

None of us had seen *Angst*, but we knew it had been a hit. And we knew a lot of the buzz centred on the show's band—Paranoia, a group that started out of a high school on the east side. We met Jane to ask about the band. She said she loved the idea. "They've got buzz."

Best of all, Dez Fiddler was willing to give us the lead singer's phone number. They were our first phone call. We didn't have plans for a second phone call. We didn't know any bands.

When we showed up at a modern duplex in a middle-class neighbourhood, Kyle and Randy and I followed the music out to someone's garage. "Not bad," said Randy as we approached. It was his kind of music—Pink Floydish.

"Not that tight," said Kyle, who'd actually sung with bands.

I didn't say anything. I wasn't listening to what they were playing and singing, I was trying to hear them playing and singing our stuff. And in my head it all sounded pretty cool.

I'd never met musicians before, so I didn't realize these guys were typical—four high school geeks who'd probably never get laid if they didn't form a band. The broody, sensitive, androgynous guy was singing about how women didn't understand him, the longhaired dude was Van Halen-ing on guitar, the wiry guy with the weird glasses was whaling away anonymously on the bass and the hefty dude was camped out behind the drum kit.

When we walked in they didn't look up and didn't stop playing. They called themselves "prog rock" which I'd later discover was music slang for "We can't write anything catchy." Not looking at us was prog attitude. They finally acknowledged us when the song skidded to a finish and they struck we-don't-give-a-shit-about-you-please-love-us poses. I clapped. It seemed polite. They looked at me like I'd missed the whole point.

"We don't play for audiences," said Gord, their bass player. "We play for the music."

Randy and Kyle and I exchanged a look. The look should have said, "Run." It didn't.

"Cool," said Randy.

"Gord," said Gord. Then he introduced us to the team. Brendan was the broody singer. Rafe "short for Rafael" was the would-be guitar god. Colin was the drummer. Then they opened a cooler and took out four cans of beer.

Gord told us he wrote most of the music. "We all write the lyrics," said Gord. "We all have something to say."

"Yeah man," said Rafe. "We got a statement to ... No, not a statement, more like a manifesto."

"Yeah," said Colin.

Brendan brooded.

"We're writing our own lyrics," I said. "We've got eight songs."

The other guys in the band all looked to Gord. It was an easy enough look to read. He was supposed to tell us to die. Gord was sizing us up. "We're not a theatre band," he said. "But Dez said we should talk to you. So, what's your show about?"

"Is it political?" asked Rafe hopefully.

Colin had a different question. "How much can you pay?"

Randy explained what the show was about and how everyone

involved was going to be rich and famous. Kyle told them the show was going to tour. But Colin just repeated his question. "How much?" All we could tell them was what we'd told everybody—that when we made money we'd share it. We'd never talked about how we'd split it—it was a given that Randy and Kyle and I would get the biggest share, but we were all going to be rich.

The band wasn't impressed. "We play bars," said Gord.

"Yeah," said Colin. "We're professional."

"But we don't need you onstage," said Randy. "We're doing a soundtrack. Like a movie."

"Recording?" said broody Brendan, who lifted his eyes from the ground so we could see he was wearing mascara. "In a recording studio?"

I'd been afraid to tell them that. I figured the only reason anybody performed in a band was for the chance to play live, but the musicians huddled around each other muttering, arguing, clearly intrigued.

Randy, Kyle and I retreated to our own corner of the garage, next to the bicycles.

"A thousand dollars," said Gord. He'd broken free of their scrum. "We want a guarantee. One thousand dollars."

A thousand dollars. I could see Kyle doing the math in his head. I was already doing the math in mine. A thousand dollars sounded okay. "No," said Randy. "Nobody else is getting a guarantee. We can't give one to you."

"Too bad," said Gord.

Randy didn't flinch. "Too bad."

We were almost out the door when Kyle mentioned that Rainbow was producing.

I couldn't see their jaws drop, but I could hear it. Suddenly the four of them were scrambling over each other to offer us beer from their cooler.

"I know a great sixteen-track studio out in Surrey. Just forty bucks an hour."

I had no idea what a track was. But sixteen sounded like plenty. And forty dollars didn't sound like anything at all. The songs were only going to be maybe three minutes each. Eight songs. Three minutes each. Even if they had to do them all three times, I figured the band would be done in an hour, two max. "Cool," I said.

"We're in," said Colin.

Rafe passed us beer cans. Randy passed them a joint. We sat on the shag rug that was on the floor to muffle the sound while Gord told us about their manifesto.

19

Driving Age

None of us would have guessed Annie's age. No one ever did. And Randy didn't know until the afternoon he saw her waiting for the bus after rehearsal and invited her to hang out. "I probably shouldn't," said Annie.

Randy looked at her like he understood. "Yeah. You're right."

"I mean, I've got a boyfriend. Shawn."

Randy nodded sympathetically. "I can respect that."

"Thanks," she said.

"Why don't you have a car?" he asked.

Annie giggled. "I'm not old enough to drive." Driving age in BC: sixteen.

"Oh," said Randy. Then, "No way!"

"How old did you think I was?"

Randy had been charming women long enough to know there was never a correct answer to this question. "Old enough to have fun," he said.

"Exactly right," she said.

Then he had to guess, just to be sure what he'd gotten himself into. "Fifteen," he said hopefully.

"And a half," she said.

"Great," said Randy. The half helped. Sort of.

When Randy told Kyle and me the news, he started with, "You're never gonna believe this." And we didn't. We couldn't. She couldn't be.

"How are we supposed to go on tour with a fifteen-year-old star?" asked Kyle.

"She's still perfect," said Randy.

"I'm with Randy," I said. "She's the best actress we saw. She nailed both parts, she looks amazing, she's dying to do it."

"But she's fifteen," said Kyle. "Am I seriously supposed to do a love scene with a fifteen-year-old?"

Randy replied, deadpan. "Are you seriously saying you wouldn't want her?"

"We could ask her parents," I said.

"Ask them what," asked Kyle. "Whether I can neck with her onstage?"

"You don't make out with her," I said. "She tries to seduce you, but you only make out with Gamatria, and she's older than you."

This seemed to relax Kyle a bit.

"I was just thinking when we tour we can ask them for permission," I said. "Kids can tour with their parents' permission, right? The same way kids do movies."

"Right," said Randy. "We can ask her parents."

Dougie was also full of surprises. One Monday when we were sitting around before rehearsal talking about our weekend, Dougie matter-of-factly told us his fun-time highlight had been "kicking the shit" out of some guys in the park. Kyle nodded and grunted at Dougie like he kicked guys in the park all the time, too. Kyle explained to me later that the steel-toed boots Dougie wore were called "shit-kickers." After Dougie was done talking about getting his kicks I told everyone to focus on the script. About twenty minutes into our run-through, Dougie grunted and got this queasy look on his face. "I can't say this," he said.

"Why not?"

"It takes the Lord's name in vain."

"It what?"

"You talk about ..." He whispered the word so we could barely hear him, "Satan."

None of us had a clue what he was talking about.

"The Devil," said Dougie, growing frantic. "Aren't you worried?"

"About what?" asked Kyle.

I knew some church people had protested *The Life of Brian* for blasphemy. Maybe Dougie thought people would protest our show because we talked about the Devil? Maybe they'd protest our show and we'd be controversial and end up on TV and sell a million tickets? Maybe he was worried about ...

"Our souls," said Dougie. "Our eternal souls."

I'd been worried about a lot of things. Heck, I thought I'd worried about *everything*. Would the show be any good? Would anyone see it? Would I ever lose my virginity? But this was new. I hadn't worried at all about the Devil. I wasn't sure Jews even believed in the Devil. I knew about Satan from movies and comics, not synagogues or Hebrew school.

"I'm a *Christian*," said Dougie. And he said the word with italics, like it was news. I knew plenty of Christians—most of whom only went to church for weddings, funerals and midnight mass. So I knew there were Catholics and Protestants and Anglicans and United— which seemed to be the Christian combo platter. I also knew plenty of Jews, even a few *Jews* in italics and yarmulkes, but I'd never met a *Christian*.

"It's just a play," I said.

Dougie stared at me. At first I thought he was angry, but he seemed genuinely concerned. "Are you a Christian?"

"No," I said. "I'm Jewish." I thought the fact we were rehearsing in the Jewish Community Centre might have been a clue. As soon as

I answered, I wondered if this meant Dougie had to use his boots on me. I think he was wondering the same thing.

"This character, Santar. He's worshipping ..." He wouldn't even say the word.

"But he's the bad guy," I said. "And this is the first of three parts."

"What happens in the next part?"

"The good guy kicks the shit out of him," said Kyle.

Dougie considered. "I guess that's okay, then."

We set a rehearsal for 7:30 the next night and I arranged to meet Heidi earlier in the afternoon. It wasn't a date. It was a meeting.

She wanted to talk about the show, go over the notes, draw up a proper props list. She suggested we meet at her house in Kitsilano. She lived a few blocks from the beach, not too far from Randy's apartment. Between the time she answered the door and the time we sat down in the living room, I learned that Heidi's dad was out of town and her mother was at work until seven. It was 4 p.m. It wasn't a date. It was a meeting. That's what I told myself when she asked if I wanted anything from her dad's liquor cabinet.

It was the kind of cozy bungalow built back when people used to build places called "cozy bungalows," and it had a small living room at the front of the house with a view of the tree-lined street. I said I was fine with Coke and she disappeared into the kitchen, brought back a Coke and an empty glass and poured herself something from the liquor cabinet. Then she reminded me we had the house all to ourselves for the next few hours.

Yes, it was just a meeting and as she settled onto the couch only a few inches away from me and said, "I really like working with you," I thought there was a good chance that when the meeting was over I was no longer going to be a virgin. Even I knew these had to be signals. I figured I'd better say something about the show, but she didn't want to talk about the show yet. She asked about me. What was my school like? How was my grad? Where was I going to university? What was

I going to study? How many plays had I written? How many had I directed? Had I ever done magic myself? Did I have a girlfriend?

She smiled when I answered the last with an embarrassed, "No."

"I didn't think so," she said.

And she laughed when I told her that because I'd gotten so far behind in my school work I was so exhausted at my grad that after I got home from the party, I slept until 8 p.m. the next night.

"Was your grad date pretty?" she asked.

"Yeah," I said. "But she had a boyfriend."

Our school had a policy that grad dates were chosen by lottery to make sure everyone had a partner, so most students arrived with their lottery partner, and left with their boyfriend or girlfriend.

"That's sad," she said, "but kinda sweet." Then she leaned in toward me and even though I hadn't kissed a girl since making out with the French ambassador I was pretty sure I remembered what I was supposed to do next as ...

The phone rang.

We froze like we'd been busted by the cops.

"I'd better get it," said Heidi. "Could be Dad."

It wasn't Dad. I couldn't figure out who it was, because I'd never witnessed a phone conversation like this one before—not in real life, just on TV. Heidi kept cycling through "Yes," and "Uhhuhuhuh," and "Are you sure?" and then, when she hung up, she started to cry.

She choked out the words, "my mother." I was trying to figure out what her mother had said to make her cry like this. I had no problem imagining mythic battles and interlocking hell dimensions and illusions where people burst into flames. But all I could picture now was that Heidi was in trouble for something, maybe for having a guy over, until she sobbed out the words, "Heart attack."

Heart attack?

"VGH. Emergency."

VGH. Vancouver General Hospital. "I'll drive you," I said. "Let's go."

We started to the door, then she stopped and grabbed the phone. "I'd better call Brian," she said.

"Is that your brother?" She hadn't mentioned a brother.

"My boyfriend. He's in the army."

The signals had gone from bright green to solid red.

Twenty minutes later we arrived at VGH. I'd never seen anyone in an oxygen mask before. And if you'd asked me, I never would have believed that someone with an oxygen mask would be allowed to smoke. But Heidi's mom, who looked to be in her mid-forties, was in the bed—looking like, well, someone who'd just had a heart attack—and she was taking turns puffing away on a cigarette and gasping air through her inhaler.

There was only one chair, so I sat on the window ledge. Heidi took the chair, talked to her mom, stared at her mom, cried, stopped crying, told her mom to put the cigarette down and cried again when the soldier walked in and hugged her. I figured this was my cue to exit. I had almost made it to the elevator when Heidi caught up with me. "I really appreciate you driving me here."

"It's okay," I said.

"I think, I mean, the show, I ..."

"Don't worry about it," I said. "We'll be okay. And if you want to help later, when your mom's better, when you're up to it ..."

"Thanks," she said. Then she hugged me and gave me a peck on the cheek before turning back to her mom's hospital room.

When I got home there was a coat hanger on the hall door. I was becoming friends with all the late-night waitresses at Denny's.

The next night after rehearsal I told Randy and Kyle what had happened. They couldn't stop laughing. "So what are you gonna do for a second date?" asked Kyle. "Kill her dad?"

I was less amused. "It's not funny. Her mom could die."

"It is funny," said Randy. "Not the dying mom part, but the boyfriend in the army. You went after a girl whose boyfriend has a gun."

Then Jane appeared. She'd met up with us almost every week to see how things were going. Randy would do a magic trick or two, say something suggestive and she'd shoot him down. For today's trick he shredded a newspaper and then, with a flick of the wrist, made it re-appear in one piece.

"That should be in the show," said Jane.

"I don't think there are newspapers in Medemptia," said Randy.

After the trick she talked about the marketing plan and told us where Rainbow would be putting ads and posters and who she want-ed to line up interviews with for us. Then she said she had big news: "We got you Robson Square."

Robson Square? It was new. It was beautiful. It was downtown and upscale with a skating rink, two movie theatres and a food fair.

"It's perfect," said Randy.

"The woman who runs it is a total Gorgon. But don't worry. I'll make sure you never have to deal with her. She's my problem."

"Great," I said.

"August tenth to fifteenth." So we had less than two months to get this together. "And it's only five hundred a night," she said.

Randy and I exchanged looks. Why did we care how much it cost to rent the theatre?

"Don't worry," she said. "You don't have to pay right away."

We had to pay? For the theatre? Didn't they pay for the theatre?

"And that covers tech, too. Plus a full day of rehearsal. "So that's three thousand for a five-day run, plus the rehearsal day. Not bad, eh?"

It sounded great. As Jane told us about Robson Square, Kyle doo-dled on one of the napkins. When he slid his drawing across the table, Randy and I said "Wow" in sync.

Jane nodded and smiled.

Kyle had sketched a pair of sexy women on either side of a helmet-ed Santar, who was leaning on a broadsword. It looked exactly like a James Bond opening credit sequence—or what a James Bond credit sequence would look like for a sword and sorcery movie.

We loved it.

"I figure we get the girls to do a pose like that," he said.

"Perfect," said Jane. Kyle beamed. He wasn't just an actor now, he was an artist. He'd designed our poster.

"When do you think they'll do the photo shoot?" I asked.

"Soon," said Jane. "This'll be great. This'll sell some tickets."

20

Running with the Devil

Until Dougie's revelation, I'd almost forgotten we had a scene with Satan. Santar was ruler of his own dimension, but since it was a hell dimension we'd figured Satan was still his boss. It was solid horror-fantasy logic. The idea was that Santar would summon Satan out of the "sceptre of the solid flame." I had no idea what "solid flame" was, but tell me that doesn't sound totally Jack Kirby cool.

We'd do the illusion with a blast of fire from an altar I'd seen in my book on ancient Egyptian magic. The Egyptians used smoke and incense. We didn't need the incense, but we could get some dry ice and hook up a smoke machine, Randy would set red lights inside it, we'd add a bit of reverb for a voice that would blast out of the speakers—Randy's voice—and then onto the next big trick.

Then Randy had a dream. He woke up and told me he'd seen the devil, our devil, and he wanted to write the lyrics for a song. So far we'd talked about some of the hook lines for the lyrics, but I'd written all the songs. But Randy had a catchphrase he wanted to try out on me, the phrase from his dream: "Lead me to Lucifer." It was like something Styx would have done if Ozzy Osbourne bit the head off Dennis DeYoung. More an incantation than a song. And a long one. Led Zeppelin-long.

"It's kinda cool," I said. "But where do we put it? The songs are there to cover the illusions and there's no magic for the Satan scene."

"No problem," said Randy. "We're gonna put a new illusion in the show." Then he presented the next idea with a magician's flourish. "I'm gonna make Satan."

Make Satan? How do you make Satan? "I thought we were just gonna do a fire trick and let people imagine ..."

"You gotta let me do this," he said, pouting. "It's my show."

It was but ... I couldn't picture it. "You can't show the Devil. The alien in *Alien* was a lot scarier before we saw it on screen. *Jaws* was scariest before we saw the fish attached to the fin. Satan's only scary because everyone has their own image of the Devil. What are we gonna do? Put a guy in a costume?"

"I'm gonna build him." Randy was still revving up. He hadn't looked this excited since we'd made the deal with Jane.

"You can really do this?" Randy looked wounded for a moment, but only for a moment.

"Nooooo problemmm. I'm gonna get a bear's skull. A grizzly bear's skull."

That sounded ... cool. Creepy, but cool.

Then he reached under the bong table to show me something he'd been hiding all afternoon. "The sculptor just finished it."

It was Santar's helmet.

"She tossed two others that she didn't think were good enough. She says she spent more on materials than we paid her to design it because she likes the idea of seeing her work onstage. Isn't it amazing?"

Up close it looked like painted plaster, but from even a few feet away it looked like hammered gold. It was awesome.

"Here, try it."

Before I could object Randy had already plunked it on my head. There was foam inside. It was comfortable. And I could see everything. "It's perfect," I said.

"I said she could have tickets to the show, too."

This was a good day. We didn't have any illusions yet, but we had our most important costume piece.

When we got to the JCC, Randy presented the helmet to Kyle like a crown at a coronation.

Kyle stared at it like it was diseased. "You want me to wear *this*?"

Randy's smile vanished faster than a coin in a palm pass. "Santar wears a helmet," said Randy. "Like Vader. It says so in the script."

"Except for the scene with Satan," I said. "You'll take it off to show your respect. That's when we'll see all the scars."

"Try it on," said Randy.

The helmet slid on like it was built for him—which it was.

"Nice," said Randy.

"You look like a Viking warrior," said Ivy.

"It really looks like gold," said Annie.

You could see Kyle's eyes through the helmet—and they weren't happy. "It's too tight," he said through the plaster.

"We can talk about it later," I said.

As Kyle handed the helmet back to Randy, it didn't look like he'd ever want to talk about it.

But now that Randy was in the room with us, I had a bigger worry. We still didn't know how Ivy was going to kill Dougie.

She couldn't light him on fire. That was way too expensive.

"Maybe we should use the guillotine," said Kyle.

It seemed logical. After all, we had a guillotine. But this was the big time and that meant we were going to do bigger, flashier illusions. The only way we could use a guillotine for *The Initiation* was if we could build one out of metal with a blade that was sharp enough to slice someone's head off. As appealing as that was, it was too expensive.

Randy wanted Ivy to stab Dougie through the heart. "So Dougie would be standing there—in a trance—and Gamatria takes Santar's sword and wham, right through the heart." This plan called for a sword made out of very flexible metal and a gizmo—a curved tube—that would be moulded to his body. Randy had seen the trick in a cata-logue and was sure he could duplicate it. He was ready to order the sword when he told me how the trick worked. "So Ivy has to stab him in precisely the right spot?"

"Yeah," said Randy, excited.

"What if she misses?"

Randy was outraged. "She won't miss. How can she miss?"

"Because he's standing. And she has to stab him quickly."

"She can set the tip over his heart, hold it there. She's supposed to hesitate, right?"

"Yeah," I said, trying to picture it. "But if she has to slide the tip of a metal blade into a metal tube that's right over his heart ... while he's standing?"

Now Randy pictured it. His smile vanished. We obviously had the same picture. This had to happen fast or people would realize the sword had roughly the same tensile strength as tinfoil.

"Maybe she should just slit his throat," I said. "We could have lots of blood."

Randy scowled. "That's not an illusion. That's a ..." he could barely say it, "special effect." Special effects artists may like to say what they do is magic, but magicians do not esteem special effects.

Kyle had a better idea. "What if he's lying down? We'll see the sword go through him. Like the guillotine."

Randy interrupted. "Not like the guillotine. It'll go right through his chest, right through the table. It'll be amazing. And we can use the same gimmick as the sword through the heart. It'll be easy to place the tip of the sword in the cylinder if he's lying down."

That made sense. "We should chain him down though," I said.

"We don't need chains," said Randy. "He's in a trance."

"Yeah, I know but chains look cool. Lying on a table is boring, chaining someone—that's classic."

Randy couldn't argue with that, "Okay, we'll chain him. And we'll use the guillotine table for rehearsal."

I still needed some magic to rehearse with. I asked Randy what he was working on.

"The floor," he said.

The floor? "I'm pretty sure the theatre's got a floor," I said. "I'm willing to bet that every theatre we go to will have a floor."

"We need trap doors, we need a place to run wires, we need to build our own floor," said Randy. "And even if the theatre we get here has a floor that works how do we know the theatres we tour to will have a floor that works?"

I had no answer for this one. "I need to start rehearsing with the magic. I need the cast to feel comfortable working with all the tricks. Can I at least get something next week?"

"No problem," said Randy.

My problem was Dougie. Dougie couldn't act. He could scream, but he couldn't act. No matter how many times we played the scene, I never believed he was remotely scared of Gamatria and he looked even less scared of our nigh-omnipotent evil overlord, Santar.

The fact that we were still rehearsing with a plastic sword I'd borrowed from the daycare didn't help, but still …

"This is a dream. This has to be some kind of dream," said Dougie as Ivy finished chaining him to the guillotine table.

"This is no dream," said Ivy. And she said it pretty convincingly.

"Okay, yeah," said Dougie. The dialogue was a little more complex in the original script, but since casting Dougie I'd trimmed it to "Okay, yeah."

Ivy held the sword above his chest and Kyle walked toward him—a menacing demigod with feathered blond hair. "You will obey her."

And that's when Dougie started to giggle. Ivy—not Gamatria—looked ready to stab him. "I am so sick of this."

Kyle scowled, but he didn't say anything. He didn't have to. He was ready to shish kebab Dougie, too—ideally with something a lot more lethal than a plastic sword.

"Sorry," said Dougie. But he didn't stop laughing.

I was the director; it was obviously time to direct. "You're supposed to scream here. You're supposed to beg for help."

"Sorry, man." He stopped laughing, but Ivy was still fuming. So were Kyle and Annie.

"You don't like the line? I'll change the line. What do you want to say?"

"That's not it," said Dougie. "It's just that—you know."

"We'll have a real sword," I said.

"Look at me," said Dougie and he sat up on the bench exposing his pecs and his pre-scarred chest.

He'd lost all of us now.

"I could kill him easy."

Before Kyle could object, I stepped in. "He's the most powerful evil sorcerer in the universe."

"I could bench-press Kyle."

"I don't think so," said Kyle.

Dougie tried to step back across the macho Maginot line. "No offence, man."

This was not going well. "We're acting, okay? Act like you're afraid of him. Places!"

Everyone went back to their places. I figured I'd jump ahead and have Kyle pick up the scene with his next line: "By the time I'm done with you, you will beg for death."

Dougie started to laugh again. "Sorry, man."

Now Kyle looked dangerous.

"Can I go for a smoke?" asked Annie.

I had to do something. I called Ivy over, slipped into the hall and told her to do the scene again, but this time to use the locks on our chains. "Do them up slowly, pretend there's music playing, and make sure you lock the stockade to hold his neck in place." Ivy didn't know there was a latch for a lock. I did. I'd locked Randy in, at least I pretended to since we'd just used the stocks to hold his Styrofoam head in place. I told her where to look. When we stepped back into the room, Kyle was still glaring at Dougie. Dougie was still smirking.

Ivy started chaining Dougie and he kept smirking as she clicked all four locks shut. Ivy and Kyle delivered their lines flatly, rote. There was no point in performing since Dougie wouldn't shake the image of how much tougher he was than Kyle.

"By the time I'm done with you, you will beg for death," Kyle said again, sounding like he meant it.

Dougie giggled again. I told Ivy she forgot his neck and she put Dougie's head through the stocks and locked him in place.

Dougie was still laughing.

Ivy and Kyle were ready to end the scene, maybe end the show, but I told them not to. "You're supposed to leave the victim alone to consider his fate. Go."

Kyle and Ivy did a double take.

"In character. Go."

Dougie stopped laughing.

"You too," I said to Annie. "Out."

"I thought I stayed," said Annie. "In the script ..."

"This time you go," I said.

As Annie started to the door, Dougie stopped smiling. "What do you think you're doing?"

"Okay, Dougie. See, here's the thing. I really think you can act. I think you can be amazing, but you've gotta get it into your head that somebody can be smaller than you and still be dangerous. It's time to get into character."

"Then why lock me up?"

"You don't look scared yet."

He started to tug at his chains. His arms moved a bit. His neck didn't. "Hey, I can't move my neck." He wasn't scared, but he wasn't amused.

"We'll come back when you sound scared."

Dougie started writhing around on the table, trying to pull loose. One of his legs came free. The table started to shake. "You're gonna flip it," I said. And if he kept moving, he would. He could probably get out, but he'd have to tip the table over and smash into the floor to do it, maybe break a few bones in the process.

He started swearing, screaming, jerking around. The table started to tip. I steadied it. "I said scared, not angry."

It was a good thing his leg was free, not his hand, because I'm pretty sure a free hand would have reached up and crushed my larynx. But he wasn't going to risk kicking me and having the guillotine tip—though I'm sure he thought about it when I walked out the door and shut it behind me.

He started screaming again.

I opened the door. He gave me a look that said this was my last day on earth.

"Scared," I said. "Not angry." Then I flicked the light switch off. "See you tomorrow." And I pulled the door shut behind me.

I couldn't see his face with the lights off, but I'm thinking that's when he must have started to look just a little bit nervous.

I joined the rest of the cast outside the daycare, on the JCC's back lawn. They'd all forgotten to light their cigarettes.

"I'm gonna kill you. I'm gonna kill you all. Annieeeee!!!" I'm not fond of exclamation marks, but you really could hear them and I'm pretty sure there were more than three, so I think I'm being pretty subdued here.

Fortunately for us, not many people were at the JCC that Sunday and I suspect anyone who was around wasn't likely to be tempted into the room by Dougie's steady stream of swearing. Even if they did go in, I had all the keys. If anyone else wanted to get him loose, they'd have to call a locksmith, or saw the table in half.

Kyle, Annie and Ivy were supposed to be smoking but they were staring at me instead. "What do you want us to do?" asked Annie.

"I thought you wanted a smoke. I'm gonna get a Coke," I said. And I did. I didn't even turn back to see if anyone was watching me cut through the parking lot toward the store.

When I came back we could still hear Dougie's screams through the window. Since he was still shouting the exact same thing it was possible he'd escaped and been replaced by a tape recorder, but if he'd escaped I was pretty sure I'd already be dead.

"He's gonna kill you," said Kyle.

"No," I said. "He's not." I took a sip of my Coke.

"I'm not gonna stop him," said Kyle.

Like you could, I thought.

"I'd kill you if I were him," said Kyle.

"No you wouldn't," I said.

This threw him. "Why not?"

"'Cause you really wanna act. And so does he. And once we get through this, I think he's gonna get it."

"And if he doesn't?"

In theatre we call a silence that lasts that many seconds a "beat." Actually, it went on long enough it qualified as a full-fledged Pinter pause, perhaps even a Beckett moment.

"Five years of braces right down the tubes."

Kyle laughed. Then somebody stopped Dougie's tape and, for the first time, he wasn't threatening anyone anymore. He was pleading. "Help!!! Somebody help me. Help!!!"

When we got to the door he was still pleading. "Help me! Please, somebody ..." I opened the door and flicked on the light. He was near tears. I was grinning. I had to grin because if this didn't work I was gonna find out what it felt like to have my face on the other end of those steel-toed boots. "That's great! That's amazing!"

Everybody looked stunned. Then Dougie snapped out of stunned and back into furious. He yanked at the chains so hard, I thought they were going to break. "You crazy ..." Then he stopped. "It is?"

"I knew you could do it."

"I'm gonna ... You ..."

"Places." Nobody moved. "Santar, Gamatria, Tathania—places."

They went back to their places.

"Silence, mortal," said Kyle, hitting just the line I needed.

Dougie looked terrified. "Please no," he pleaded. "I swear I'll help you. I'll do anything."

"It's too late for that," said Kyle. "Much too late."

Kyle started for the exit, and the others followed like they were supposed to. Dougie let loose with a "Nooooooo" that had enough "o"s to fill up the next few pages.

Everyone stopped dead. Ivy, God or Oryon bless her, applauded.

"Amazing," I said to Dougie. "Thank you," I whispered to Ivy.

Dougie's anger was gone, his fear was gone—they'd been replaced by something much more powerful: actor's ego. "It was pretty good, eh?"

"It was great," I said. I took the keys out of my pocket. "I'd better undo those." As I walked to the table, the mood shifted as everyone remembered I was about to die. I undid the first lock, then the second and finally, the neck brace. Even though I'd released his hands and feet I didn't look up, didn't even glance at Dougie until he shouted, "Hey."

I felt a chill. My dental work flashed before my eyes.

"Can we do it one more time?" he asked. "Just to make sure I've got it?"

"Sure," I said. "Let's go again."

And we did. But we didn't just do it once. At Dougie's request we ran the scene over and over for the next half hour.

21

General Anesthetic

I don't know exactly why I said yes to the nose job. There were a lot of reasons I wasn't getting dates in high school, but my nose wasn't in the top twenty. And if I had to name a facial feature I didn't like, I definitely would have gone for the ears. They were too big and stuck out too far. I didn't love my nose, but I hated my ears.

My nose was big and sharp, but lacked the Barbra Streisand bump that only Jews are allowed to admit makes us look Jewish. My nose didn't look WASP-y, but it didn't look Jewish. I knew this because I'd been mistaken for Greek and Italian far more often than I'd been identified as a descendant of Abraham.

But my mom had once told me if I ever wanted a nose job, she'd be happy to pay for it—and when I realized how many of my friends and relatives no longer had their original nasal equipment I thought, why not? In the 1970s it was the rite of passage a lot of Jewish kids went through sometime between their bar or bat mitzvah and first-year university. I'd agreed to do this almost a year earlier and by the time I signed on for *The Initiation* it was too late to change the date, so the best I could do was take advantage of the enforced rest.

Before I went in, I found myself telling Dr. Bob it would be nice to spend a few days in the hospital because it would be relaxing. Besides, my grandfather had always been convinced I had a problem with adenoids—whatever they were—so maybe this would help me breathe easier. And the plastic surgeon, Dr. Lewinsky, made it sound so simple, like getting a tooth pulled. For someone with a tendency to over-think things, I'd agreed to surgery with less hesitation than I agreed to pop on a beard and jump onstage as Adoma. Even when I was admitted to the hospital I still wasn't taking it seriously. And I suspect I wouldn't have been scared at all if not for my hospital roommate, James.

James, the guy in the bed next to me, was terrified.

My nose job was cosmetic surgery. James' nose job qualified as a humanitarian gesture. He was in his mid-twenties and had the smallest head I'd ever seen—almost all of it nose. He looked like Pinocchio after a long and savage election campaign. Even before James told me he was in for the same surgery with the same surgeon, I decided that if he was in for something else, anything else, I had to offer him my spot.

Unlike me, James had prepared for surgery. He'd read statistics. He knew facts. And he was terrified. So while I was lying on my hospital bed fiddling with script revisions, James was telling me exactly what the odds were of dying under general anesthetic. I didn't know you could die under anesthetic. How could anyone die doing something routine when they were in a hospital surrounded by doctors? James was convinced he was risking his life. "It's crazy," he said. "It's not like I can't breathe. What do I need a new nose for? I could die tomorrow. Or if something goes wrong during surgery—brain damage."

Brain damage?

"And do you know how painful recovery is supposed to be?"

Painful?

"Even if it goes well, we're still going to have two black eyes and be on painkillers for like a week. Maybe longer."

I hadn't paid enough attention to know there would be black

eyes—never mind pain. I didn't have time for pain. I had a show to rehearse.

For almost two hours, James regaled me with every hospital horror story he'd ever heard and then, without warning, he announced he was going to sleep. "Thanks for listening, pal. You really made me feel better."

Then he turned toward the plastic statue of Jesus writhing in agony on the cross that was stuck to the wall behind his hospital cot, started muttering what I assumed was a prayer—because he crossed himself after he finished—and passed out cold. My eyes were wide open. There was no way I was going to sleep that night. Pain? Brain damage? Death? Jesus statues? I wanted to go. Now.

The next day I took one of the script pages, wrote a note and hid it underneath my blanket, on top of my hospital gown. It read, "Do not fold, spindle or mutilate." I pulled it out just as they stuck the gas mask over my face to administer the general anesthetic.

James had mentioned a lot of potential nightmare scenarios for the surgery, but there was one that even he hadn't come up with. The surgeon had just started breaking my nose when I woke up, sat bolt upright and announced, "This isn't fun anymore, I'm leaving now. This hurts."

I can tell you exactly what it was that woke me up. But if you're squeamish, skip to the next paragraph. I heard a sound like someone biting into a Crispy Crunch bar. That sound was the bridge of my nose being broken with a surgical chisel. And, yes, I know how a Crispy Crunch bar feels when someone takes a bite out of it—which is why I still cringe when I see one at the 7-Eleven. Some people want to free lab animals, or save baby seals—every time I walk by a candy counter, I have an incredible urge to stop the suffering of the Crispy Crunches.

After announcing I was leaving, I started to get off the operating table. The next sound I heard was everyone in the operating room screaming. At least two people were shoving me down. Then they wrapped my legs and arms in surgical restraints, but I remembered my magic training and twisted and clenched my arms and wrists like I'd practised a hundred times with soft rope and chains. The anesthesiologist shoved the mask on me again. I took a deep breath and passed out. Sort of. I heard everything. I felt everything. But I couldn't move. Until the surgeon said, "That's it."

And I said, "Are we done now? That really hurt."

A woman—I'm not sure who because I couldn't quite open my eyes, shouted, "Oh my God!"

Another woman swore.

Then I flipped my wrists around—just the way I'd practised—twisted my arms out of the restraints, sat up straight, grinned and proclaimed, "Houdini was a slouch."

Everyone screamed again. And I finally passed out.

Looking back, I realize this is the type of thing lawyers live for. Except for the pain, I thought it was funny and so did all my friends.

It took so long for James to return from the operating room that I thought maybe one of his worst-case scenarios had come true. After all, if I could wake up under anesthetic—he really could die. When the nurse wheeled him back on the gurney he already looked better. Even covered with bandages his head no longer looked like it belonged on a toucan. I wanted to congratulate him. But when the nurse saw I was awake again, she upped my dosage of morphine. When you try to escape from a hospital bed while they're operating on you, they don't take any chances.

While I was out of my mind on painkillers, I repeated one word like a mantra: "Tchara."

The nurses must have thought I'd suffered that brain damage James had warned me about.

I discovered later the doctors were so upset by my escape attempt they triple-dosed me with morphine so I would definitely feel no pain. When I occasionally looked up through the haze at little tortured Jesus, I finally understood why they put the image of crucified, agonized Jesus in the rooms instead of happy, smiling, handing-out-loaves-and-fishes Jesus. This was the Christian symbol for "You think you got it bad?"

I also got why Jesus could never have been accepted as a Jewish God—because every elderly Jew I knew loved to moan about everything from their tsoris to their psoriasis and this guy would clearly steal a bit of their thunder.

When the priest came to visit I wasn't sure if it meant I was dying or if the hospital staff had decided to convert me now that I no longer had any trace of a Jewish nose. I was so out of it, they could have reattached my foreskin and I wouldn't have noticed. "You're not here for the last rites are you?"

"I'm here if you need to talk," he said.

"What do you wanna talk about?"

I'm not sure what he said, because I passed out again. And when I woke up I resumed my mysterious mantra.

"Tchara." It was the first thing I said to Randy when he came to visit. And I said it like he'd know exactly what it meant. He didn't. So I told him. Or I tried to. He told me later I pretty much kept repeating the word, "Tchara." Then he said I told him something—in gibberish—but it looked like I knew what I was saying. We needed somebody in the show to challenge Santar—an enemy—Tchara. While I was under anesthetic I'd realized we had a huge problem with the script. Santar talked a lot and everybody did a lot of tricks but nobody—even Satan—ever said much to him except, "Yes, master." We needed some conflict. There was an obvious answer ... bring back Oryon.

But we were allergic to obvious answers, so instead of bringing in our hero—who was already part of our cast—I created a tougher villain, an ex-lover. Tchara.

I had the name first, but it didn't take long to start picturing her. I kept seeing images of a girl in a sexy sorceress outfit. There was only one girl I'd ever seen who intimidated Kyle. Tabitha. I wrote the new pages in the hospital. Longhand.

I got lucky. No black eyes. And as I discovered when I moved back to Randy's two days later, I looked different but apparently not that different. At my first rehearsal back, Ivy asked if I'd gotten a haircut. Dougie thought I'd changed my glasses. They knew I'd done something ... but nobody could figure out exactly what. Then Kyle cornered me during a smoke break. "Nice nose job. Did it hurt?" Nobody else had guessed.

Who told him?

"I went out with Sheri Charko back in grade ten," he said. "She got one. You two have the same nose now." Sheri Charko had a nose job? And now we had the same nose? It turned out that my doctor, also Sheri's, had a signature style. So if someone says Jews in Vancouver look alike, they may not be anti-Semitic, they might be commenting on how many of us have Dr. Lewinsky's nose.

22

Echoes of Confusion

Someone had to scare Santar. When I told Kyle about Tchara he wasn't sold on adding a character—"We're up in less than eight weeks"—but then I showed him the new scenes. "They're good," he said. "Really good."

It wasn't a big part, but it was fun. I'd used the same premise as the victim to set up the idea that our audience was never safe. The idea was that an evil entity possessed a woman in the audience. So our Tchara would jump out of her comfy theatre seat, scream like she'd been shot and walk up to the stage in a trance. Then she'd exchange sexually charged insults with Santar, do a nasty magic trick and some prophesying and die a gruesome death because—and this was classic comic book stuff, very Dark Phoenix—the body of her puny mortal host wasn't strong enough to sustain her spirit.

Since we didn't expect the audience to suspend their disbelief enough to think we'd possessed someone with a demon, the actress playing Tchara would be billed in the program. But nobody would know there was an actress in the audience until after she'd gone onstage.

"What about Eva?" said Kyle. "She was good."

My new nose ached at the thought. I tried to sound casual. "I'd like to try Tabitha."

"Of course you would," said Kyle with a bit too much of a smirk for my liking. "You're the director."

When I called Tabitha she sounded happy to hear from me. But when I said it was about the play she sounded confused. "It's been so long, I figured you were already rehearsing."

Before I could come up with an answer, she did. "You fired someone. And now you want me. That's okay. So who am I?" she asked. "Gamatria or Tathania?"

"Neither," I said.

"But they're the only two female parts. Unless you're going with a female Santar. That would be fun."

I couldn't believe she remembered the names of all the characters. I hardly remembered the names of all the characters.

"And kinky," she said.

I don't think I'd ever heard anybody call anything "kinky" before. I really liked the way she said that.

"It's a new part," I said.

The silence was painful, awkward.

"I kind of ... wrote it for you."

I hadn't meant to say that. I definitely hadn't meant to say that. I hadn't even officially cast her yet.

She didn't laugh. She didn't say anything.

"Are you there?"

"That's sweet," she said. "That's really sweet."

Sweet? Damn. She'd called me *sweet*. But we had our Tchara.

When I got home the coat hanger was on the door again. All I wanted to do was collapse on my couch. After rehearsal I'd had to drive out to watch the band jam for three hours on a few songs that weren't sounding at all like I'd imagined them. I saw the stupid hanger, considered ignoring it or pretending our poltergeist had run off with it, then I heard the giggles from inside our place. I'd just turned to walk to Denny's when the door opened.

"Mark!" the voice was enthusiastic, perky and ...

Fifteen.

"Hey," I said to Annie, trying to keep a smile plastered on my face.

"Hey," said Annie. "Randy said you were his roomie, but I've never seen you here before."

Before? As in more than once? I didn't need to know this. I didn't want to know this.

"See you at rehearsal tomorrow," she said as she bounced out of our building.

My grin felt like the Joker's—painful and painted on. "See ya tomorrow," I said. I took the coat hanger off the door and walked inside to stab my partner with it. Randy was sitting on my bed, smoking a joint and watching a *Trek* rerun on TV. At least he was dressed. If he'd been wearing his purple Hef bathrobe ... "Hey buddy."

"She's fifteen."

Randy barely glanced at me. "And a half."

"She's our star." I remembered that's why he'd wanted her to be the star. "Hey, we just fooled around a bit ... We haven't had sex or anything."

So what did fooling around mean? I didn't need to know this. I really didn't need to know this. If Randy and Annie had a thing and it ended badly, and Randy's things always ended badly, what was I supposed to do, wear the chain-mail bra myself? "She has a boyfriend."

"Yeah, probably some pimply faced fifteen-year-old. Like I care. His name's Shawn. Seriously what's Little Shawn gonna do?"

Okay, fine, "Shawn" didn't sound all that scary, but still ... "Just ... I dunno ... if you're gonna do something stupid, can you wait until after the show?"

Now he looked up at me. I'd never called him stupid before. We'd never fought before. He got a look on his face like ...

No, it wasn't anger. I thought it was anger at first, but it was darker than that. I didn't think Randy got dark. This was Mr. No Problem. "I'm gonna tell you something and if you ever tell anyone else ... I'm gonna ... I dunno ... but you promise to never tell anyone?"

I knew what it was. "You did have sex with her?"

He smiled. "Yeah, but that's not it." He said it like he was kidding. I hoped he was kidding. Then he followed up with something that wasn't remotely funny.

"I always thought I'd be dead by now."

"That's kinda morbid." I assumed he was talking about fate or karma or some twisted premonition, but it turned out that when he was a kid he'd been out hiking and had fallen off a cliff. Really. Fallen off a cliff like the coyote in the Road Runner cartoons. He'd landed on a rock ledge and his body wasn't quite as resilient as the coyote's.

He didn't die—no surprise there—but the fact that he was still breathing stunned the fireman who carried him back up the mountain. He'd fallen far enough that the fact that he lived made the TV news. On the outside, he looked pretty good—he had cuts and scrapes and bruises, but nothing too scary. The doctors who looked inside were less impressed. He'd banged up his internal organs pretty badly and they'd either taken something out, or put something back together with Scotch tape and staples.

"That's why I can't do major escapes. I can't risk anything that puts too much pressure on my stomach."

"You could ..." I couldn't say "die." Not about someone almost my age, not when I was talking about real death as opposed to the "I'm gonna kill you" death guys joked about all the time.

"Yeah," he said.

"So it's like Houdini. One punch and you could rupture your spleen or something."

"Pretty much," he said.

I didn't know what I was supposed to say. I knew this meant ... something. I was a writer, I wanted to know what made people tick and this, this had to explain who Randy really was, what he did, why.

So I asked, "Is that why you wanna ..." I couldn't say the correct word here either. Not when it didn't apply to something like getting your leg caught in a car door, or having an asshole director chain you to a table. So I said, "hook up," instead. "With so many girls?"

Randy considered for a moment. "Hell no. That's just because I'm horny."

I didn't know what else to say, so I asked him about the illusions. "We really need to start rehearsing with them. The actors are getting nervous. So am I. We've only got six weeks."

"No problem," he said.

Then I asked how his lines were coming and if he wanted to run them.

"I'm tired," he said.

Because he was the narrator I didn't need him at many rehearsals. Besides, he had a day job.

The next day, during a cigarette break, Kyle was inhaling deeply on his Player's Light and I was enjoying the buzz of the second-hand smoke—when I decided to ask Kyle if he got why every woman but Lisa seemed willing to do the backstroke on Randy's waterbed.

"He loves them," said Kyle.

The surprise on my face asked the next question for me.

"For as long as he's with them, five seconds, five minutes, a few hours, a few days, he loves them with all his heart. It's completely sincere. Then they're gone and *pffft*." He made a sound like a cigarette butt sizzling out in a puddle. "I think he's a love bulimic."

That night, before I made my usual offer to drive everyone home, Tabitha offered to let me. She got in the passenger seat like she owned the car, like she owned me, too. "Thanks for the lift," she said. Or maybe I should say purred, because there was a spin on the way she talked to me that I'd never heard before—but it was more predatory than a purr. More like a growl.

She was scaring me the way I'd imagined her scaring Santar.

"You going home?"

I shook my head. "I gotta check on the band."

"Can I come, too?"

No one else had wanted to listen to the band. Even Randy didn't seem interested in hearing them until they finished writing his epic—*Lead me to Lucifer.* But when we arrived at the garage I could hear them singing all the way from the street ...

They were playing my song.

I'd never even imagined writing lyrics before and now this band—this real rock band—was playing my song. When I stepped into the garage and they finally finished, they were asking me whether it sounded okay. It was my song. Of course it sounded okay. It sounded amazing. It sounded just like Styx. Actually, it sounded almost exactly like Styx's *Queen of Spades.*

It was *Voices*. Gamatria's theme.

> *Reality warps around you*
> *Insanity always prevails*
> *The madness of others surrounds you*
> *You do what is right, it fails*
> *You search for alternative choices*
> *But despise the answers you find*
> *The deceit, the hatred, the voices*
> *Are taking their toll on your mind*

Tabitha smiled as they hit the chorus.

> *You can always surrender*
> *You can always give in*
> *Follow the voices*
> *Or you'll never win.*

"You wrote that?" she said.

I nodded.

"Sounds like you," she said.

This was the song that played when Gamatria was trapped in the mime cage. And looking at Tabitha's smile I suddenly got why so many guys who looked like me learned to play guitar. I wasn't just a writer anymore, I was a songwriter.

"So?" asked Gord.

"It's great."

"It's getting there," said Gord. "The next one's darker."

And they started in on the theme song for Tathania, while I watched Tabitha watching the band and Rafe and Colin and Brendan and Gord watching Tabitha. It was almost 1 a.m. when we started to drive back to the city. I asked Tabitha where she lived. "I don't want to go home yet," she said. "Do you?"

It was late but ...

"Why don't we go somewhere ... to talk."

"Like Denny's?" I asked.

"Why don't we stay in the car," she said. "Find some place to park?"

"Sure," I said.

We drove to Queen Elizabeth Park, up the hill by the Conservatory. There were no other cars. She told me she'd caused a traffic accident once.

I asked what she'd done.

She told me she'd walked down the street in shorts and a bikini top and a driver smiled at her and drove straight into a parked car. "Guys like to look at me," she said. She waited for a response, but I didn't have one. I wasn't quite sure what to say to that. "You like to look at me."

Words. I couldn't find my words. I must have left them back at the garage with the band.

"What is it with guys like you?"

"What do you mean?"

"You all want milk ad girls."

"What's a milk ad girl?"

"You know, blonde. Pretty. Perky. Safe. Someone," she said the next word like she was choking on it, "wholesome ... Girls who wear crosses between their breasts." I felt like she'd looked into my head and seen Sarah. Except Sarah wore a Star of David and ... Did she say breasts?

"Someone who can't keep up with you."

I was going to ask why girls always fell for ... whatever kind of guy Randy was ... or Sarah dated, when I snagged on something else she'd said. "What do you mean guys like me?"

"Any guy smart enough to interest me."

I should have known something like that was coming, but I didn't have a clue. She smiled at me and I think I stopped breathing. And then I couldn't breathe because her mouth was on mine. And it was abundantly clear she knew a lot more about French kissing than the ambassador from France.

This was exactly what I'd told Randy he couldn't do. And I so didn't care ...

When I dropped Tabitha off at her place she said, "This doesn't mean we're going out or anything."

"It doesn't?"

"No," she said. "But that was fun." Then she kissed me again, called me "Mr. Director" in the same breathy tones Marilyn Monroe used when she sang *Happy Birthday Mr. President* and ran up the cobblestone steps to her parents' house.

I knew this was wrong.

I'd told Randy this was wrong.

So I knew one thing for sure—I couldn't tell Randy about this.

When I got home Randy was still up watching TV, which was strange, but what was stranger was that he'd been cooking. The only thing we ever ate at the apartment was pizza—and by the time I got to try it, it was usually cold. That's why I was so excited when I saw the brownies. I sliced one, brought it out to my bed/couch and was about to bite when Randy screamed, "Don't eat that!"

Maybe I should have asked, but he never asked before eating any of the food I brought home.

"They're *special* brownies."

"What? Your mom made them or something?"

"I made them."

We'd been living together almost two months. The closest I'd ever seen Randy come to cooking was pouring milk on his Frosted Flakes.

"They're *brownies*."

I knew they were brownies.

"You can't eat these."

"There are nuts in them?" I was impressed. I was surprised he remembered I was allergic to nuts.

"They're hash," he said.

"Oh," I said. Hash? Drugs? I didn't do drugs. But I was really hungry. I took my brownie again and Randy grabbed it.

"If you wanna do drugs some day, fine, do drugs. But I'm not gonna start you on them." He held the evil brownie, the evil brownie that looked so much tastier than a Denny's bran muffin. And after my adventures with Tabitha, maybe this was just what I needed.

"It's the only food in the house."

"We've got grape jelly," he said.

Since I was fairly certain Randy hadn't bought anything else resembling food, ever, it was a safe bet the jelly had been in the fridge when he moved in.

But that night it tasted great.

23

Little Shawn

One month.

Now everyone was getting nervous.

"We're supposed to be working with fires and knives," said Ivy. "Don't we need to rehearse with them already?"

When I got home I told Randy if we didn't have magic, we at least needed a proper theatre to rehearse in. Randy called his dad and the next day we moved out of the daycare and upstairs to the auditorium. Dark magic felt a lot darker in a theatre than it did surrounded by sandboxes and stuffed animals.

Getting onstage made everything feel more real. It also reminded everyone we still didn't have a set, or props, or illusions, or costumes.

When I told Randy the team was on the verge of mutinying if I didn't bring in something magical for them to rehearse with, he announced we needed a night to relax, to get to know each other. He invited everybody but the band to Bud's.

He and I even decided to splurge and pick up the first round and the nachos. Dr. Bob didn't want to come, David was too young and Tabitha said she had plans. But everyone else was going to show up—including assorted boyfriends and girlfriends.

I didn't think we were ready to celebrate anything yet. Not only did we not have the magic, but I wasn't seeing the magic I wanted in the acting. So I agreed to the party, but only if we had a rehearsal first with my three leads. I'd pick Randy up at our apartment on the way to Bud's. We'd meet everyone else there.

I knew Kyle found Annie attractive, but they didn't have any chemistry onstage. There were sparks with Ivy, there was tension with Tabitha, but nothing with Annie since he'd discovered she was fifteen. Annie was supposed to seduce him, so he'd choose her even though Gamatria had more power and was Oryon's chosen disciple.

I called Annie aside before they went at their seduction scene that night and asked her to stay as close to Kyle as possible. "Don't be afraid to touch him," I whispered to her. I wanted the same heat they'd had in that audition. She smiled, nodded. I'd figured maybe it'd be easier for them to connect if Tabitha and Dougie weren't there to watch. If it was just the three of us. Annie took the stage. They started again and she began orbiting him, getting closer and closer.

"Santar," said Tathania, "together we can rule this universe. Every universe."

"No," said Santar.

"Remove your helmet," she said. Naturally, Kyle wasn't wearing the helmet.

"Are you attempting to seduce me?" asked the always-suspicious Santar. "Or possess me?"

Tathania moved closer, her hand touched his wrist. Kyle flinched, surprised, then he recovered his inner Santar. Tathania moved closer to him, so he could feel her breath, taste it. "I simply see no need for you to be wearing your battle helmet. I have never seen your true face."

Santar hesitated a moment, the moment I was hoping for, then pulled away. "And you never shall."

Tathania grabbed his wrist, pulled him back, looked like she was about to take him right there on the stage. "That depends—are you truly ordaining a high priestess? Or a mistress?"

Santar didn't even mime throwing off his helmet. He just pulled her toward him and his lips approached hers as ...

"What the hell is this!?"

The words shot out from behind us. We all turned to see a guy in his mid-twenties in biker leathers who looked a little too anti-social to be part of a gang.

"Uh, we're rehearsing," I said.

"I don't think so," he said. The biker started toward the stage. Our nigh-omnipotent demon lord looked ready to wet himself. As concerned as I was about our new visitor, I couldn't help thinking—if I can get him to give us that look when Satan appears, we're golden.

Just as mystery biker reached the stage, Annie leapt into his arms. His hands caught her, cradled her butt and their lips locked. When the biker monster deposited her back on the floor, Kyle introduced himself.

"I'm Kyle." Kyle extended a hand to shake.

Biker Monster looked at it for a moment, like he was deciding whether to shake it or eat it. He took it and held it.

"Good to meet you Kyle. I'm Shawn." Shawn looked meaner than Dougie. He wore the same steel-toed boots. He probably had his own knife scars. Maybe he was the one who had stabbed Dougie. I think Shawn meant to whisper what he said next, but voices carry on a stage and I was pretty sure he'd never performed before—except maybe in front of a jury. "If you ever get that close to my girl again, I'll kill you."

So this was Little Shawn ... Thank Oryon he didn't know about Randy.

Annie slipped between her co-star and boyfriend so smoothly it was like she'd rehearsed that move more than she had any scene in the play. "C'mon Shawn," she said. "Let's meet everybody else." Then she turned to Kyle. "It's okay, Shawn's just kidding."

But Shawn was still gripping Kyle's hand—tight—and he didn't have a "just kidding" look on his face. "We good?"

"Yeah," said Kyle.

"Good," said Shawn. He let go of Kyle's hand and Annie led her beau toward me. "You Randy?"

How did Little Shawn know who Randy was?

"That's Mark," said Annie.

Shawn grunted. "So Annie says we're all going for drinks?"

"Yeah," I said.

"Everybody gonna be there?"

"Dougie's gonna be there," Annie told Shawn. Then she turned my way to explain. "Shawn and Dougie are old buds." But Shawn wasn't listening to Annie. He was still looking at me, waiting for my response.

"I think so," I said. I still wasn't sure what he was getting at until he said ...

"Even the magician?"

"I think so," I said.

"Great." Then he looked at Annie. "Let's grab a smoke."

As the director, it was normally up to me to set the smoke breaks, but if Shawn and Annie needed to smoke, I wasn't going to object. Though I was going to make sure Randy wasn't at Bud's that night.

I didn't say "I told you so," but when I got to our apartment I had to say something. "He's bigger than Dougie."

Randy looked like a vampire had drained every ounce of his blood. "I have to go," he said. "It's my show."

"I'll tell them you're working on the magic. It's not like we don't need the magic."

"I have to go," he said again, his voice dead. "It's my show."

"He'll kill you."

"Maybe you're wrong," he said. "Maybe he doesn't know."

"You don't wanna do this."

"I have to," he said. "We'll go together." Then he put his suit jacket on over his T-shirt.

I'd seen *High Noon* and suddenly going to Bud's that night felt a lot more Tex than Mex.

One of the reasons I'm convinced there are more than just five senses is that I don't believe there is anyone who can't sense trouble. I felt it as soon as I parked the car, opened the door and heard the music. It was the same music they always played at Bud's, but it seemed angrier, more disturbing. When Randy and I opened the Old West-style swinging doors it had transformed from a fun place to hang out, drink cider and eat nachos to a brawl waiting to happen.

Annie was already there. She was sitting with Shawn. Ivy was next to Dougie. He hadn't brought a date, but he was seriously flirting with a waitress, so he wasn't planning on going home alone.

Kyle was talking about an audition he'd done for a commercial. He'd had a callback. They had him do an Irish accent. He loved doing accents. He was snuggled up next to his girlfriend, Wendy.

Randy walked in like a sheriff who'd been challenged by the Clanton Gang. But he didn't look like the sheriff who saved the day, he looked like the one who got bullets shot at his feet and had to dance for the guys in the black hats before they put him out of his misery and the hero rode into town to avenge his dead brother.

Shawn glanced up from his drink. He didn't look at Randy, he shot Cyclops-style beams at him with his eyes. Randy grabbed a seat, ordered a margarita, told a lame joke to Belushi and was about to show Ivy how he could make a salt shaker pass through our table when Shawn pushed back his chair with the practised ease of a seasoned barroom brawler. From the confused looks on all the other faces it was clear that other than Shawn and Annie, only Randy and I knew what this was about. Everyone was looking at Shawn like he'd lost his mind.

"We didn't really do anything," said Annie trying to be helpful. She wasn't. "It was no big deal." Now everyone was looking at Randy the same way I had when I saw Annie leaving our apartment.

"She's fift ..." Kyle started, then stopped himself. The age issue wasn't exactly the point. Shawn was older than all of us.

Randy didn't attempt a denial, just an apology. "I didn't know she had a guy," he lied. "I wouldn't have ..."

Shawn glared at him across the table. "I'm gonna kill you."

As mad as he was, I was pretty sure Shawn wasn't talking "kill" as in Randy would never breathe again. By "kill" I figured he meant what teenage boys and hockey players usually meant. He was gonna mess Randy up. Maybe he'd bust his nose, maybe he'd knock out some teeth. Maybe, just maybe, he'd bust a rib or two. But I realized that with Randy's insides, if Shawn did what he was planning to do, he probably would kill him—for real. If the wrong escape trick could kill Randy, what would a kick in the ribs with a steel-toed boot do?

My nose still hurt when I sneezed, but I was willing to bet that just as surely as noses could be reset, internal organs couldn't. So that's when I did what was probably the most dangerous thing I'd done in my life. I stood up and said, "No."

Shawn stared at me like the idiot I was. Then he laughed. "You gotta be kidding."

Annie watched Shawn, but she didn't move. Her eyes said she was sorry. At least that's what I thought they said. Having seen a lot more bar brawls since then—almost all of them featuring guys like Shawn with girls like Annie—I wonder now if her eyes were actually saying, "Isn't it awesome my guy will rip someone's lungs out of his eye sockets for me? Isn't he just the dreamiest?"

My nose was talking too—but just to me. It was saying, "Remember the Crispy Crunch bar?" But as much as I wanted to follow my nose, I couldn't shake the vision of whatever was broken inside Randy's stomach collapsing like Houdini's spleen.

"He's sorry, he was stupid, it won't happen again."

"No shit."

Shawn took another step forward. I'm sure the music in the bar was still playing, but I couldn't hear it.

Randy stood—sort of. "It's okay," he said. "He's right."

"Let's forget all this and we'll buy you a drink, okay?" I said.

He wasn't listening. Randy wasn't running. Shawn was now close enough to punch Randy—if he could punch through me.

"Out of my way," he said.

All I could hope for now was that after Shawn rebroke my nose, Randy would regain his senses long enough to run. "I'm gonna make him pay," Shawn said.

"No," I said. I'd like to say it was a great western moment, pure Eastwood, but even as I said the word all I could think of was how much this was gonna hurt.

Shawn no longer found me amusing. "You gonna stop me?"

Not likely, I thought, but I had to try. I was braced for impact when I heard the words, "I will." It was Kyle. Somehow he'd magically appeared beside me.

"Me too," said Dougie. He had a hand on Shawn's shoulder.

Shawn glared at Dougie. "You don't wanna do this."

"Nope," said Dougie. "But I will."

It looked like the only two guys at the table who knew how to fight were going to go at it when Belushi appeared, holding a wooden chair at about the same level as Shawn's head. "Out. All of you." I hadn't noticed it before, but Belushi looked tough enough to take out Shawn and Dougie—especially with that chair in his hands.

Shawn grunted, then kicked over his chair, grabbed Annie by the arm and told her they were going. Annie chirped a few goodbyes like it was a typical night out—and I suspect it was—and they were gone.

I thanked Dougie while Kyle thanked Belushi and asked for another round for the table. "You got ID?" Belushi asked. Kyle stammered something about leaving it at home. "Pay the bill. I don't wanna see you here again. Any of you."

Kyle was still staring at Belushi like he'd been dumped by a lover when Randy shyly approached Dougie to thank him.

"I wasn't gonna help *you*," he said. "I just wasn't gonna let him hurt Mark."

I was touched. Randy wasn't.

"And if Annie quits cause you couldn't keep your hands off her— I'll kill you myself."

I thanked Dougie again and, once we were out in the parking lot, thanked Kyle. "Randy deserved that," Kyle said. "Why'd you get up?"

I couldn't tell Kyle, I'd promised. "I was hoping it might stop the fight," I said. "Why'd you get up?"

Kyle stared at me in disbelief. "Do you know what that guy coulda done to your nose?"

"Yeah, I guess if he hit me he would have broken it again."

"Broken it? The cartilage in there is so soft right now if he hit you in the face, he probably would have killed you." Kyle practically whispered the next words: "You could have died ... for real."

I'm proud to say I didn't faint.

24

Press Released

Our big night out had not been the morale booster we'd been hoping for. On the bright side, Annie showed up the next day.

But instead of being impressed by my courage, there was a sense from Kyle and Dougie and even Ivy that I'd gotten in the way of a righteous and honourable beating. I couldn't explain why I'd done it without betraying Randy's secret. I tried to make it clear that I wasn't impressed with Randy's behaviour either. "I was just hoping to stop a fight. This is Randy's show," I said. "He's the magician."

Even Kyle didn't seem sold on that anymore. "So where's the magic?"

The actors wanted to see the illusions. Of course they wanted to see the illusions. They wanted to rehearse with them. Now everyone knew their lines and knew the blocking—sort of. There was no way to be sure how accurate anything was yet because everything was supposed to be choreographed to go with the music and the magic and the set and we still didn't have any of those things—though Randy kept assuring me we would any second now. And we couldn't do too much work on artsy stuff like motivations because everyone's real motivation was to do cool tricks that would blow the audience's minds.

"You said we'd have the tricks by now," said Annie.

"They're supposed to be here," I said.

"I want to use the sword already," said Ivy. "I want to be comfortable with it before we open."

"And what about the fire pond?" asked Tabitha. "If I'm supposed to come out of a wall of fire I want to make sure I don't burn the place down."

"Randy's working on it," I said.

"This is bullshit," said Kyle. "How are we supposed to rehearse a magic show without magic tricks?"

Et tu Santar?

It was a mutiny. I had to do something. Fast.

I asked Kyle for a cigarette. Everyone was thrown. Kyle was the one who said, "You don't smoke," but everyone was thinking it.

Tabitha tossed me a cigarette and smiled at me like she knew what I was up to. That was impressive, since I didn't know what I was up to. I smiled at her, she smiled back and I had to break eye contact while I still could. I'd had a cigarette once—when I was five. I'd asked my father what it tasted like. "Is it more like chocolate or strawberry?" I'd figured anything that addictive had to taste like one or the other. At five I hadn't even branched out into Coke yet. The only good flavour I knew for pop was orange. My father said I should try his. I put it in my mouth, sucked on it to get at that yummy flavour and coughed until I thought I was going to throw up. This was the first time I'd even touched a cigarette since the day I discovered they tasted like smoke.

I held Tabitha's cigarette and stared at it. Annie offered me her lighter. I declined. I wasn't going to light it. I stared at it like I was going to ignite it with my eyes—like it was a magic trick. Then I sat on the edge of the JCC stage and started plucking out the pieces of tobacco one by one.

Nobody was talking now. They just stared at the director who had lost his mind. I'm not sure how long they were quiet—if you really need to know, buy a Player's Light and see how long it takes you to re-move each strand of tobacco, one at a time, without tearing the paper. When I was done I put the empty cigarette casing down on the table and told everyone I had an idea.

We'd done every acting exercise I'd ever tried or heard of. But they were right, what we needed was magic. But we didn't have it. I'd told everyone how dangerous the illusions would be and how much we needed to practise with them and here we were, a few weeks from opening, and the only trick we'd been able to rehearse was Ivy's mime cage—the only trick that didn't require magic. And we couldn't even rehearse that properly because she was supposed to be working with lighting effects and music.

"Let's run this like there isn't going to be any magic."

It took a moment for this to register.

"Isn't that what we're doing now?" asked Annie.

"No," I said. "Right now we're faking the magic. Let's start block-ing the whole thing so that if the magic doesn't show up, we still have a show."

"The magic is going to show up, isn't it?" asked Kyle.

"Of course it is," I said. "But this is theatre. It's live. Just in case something goes wrong ..."

No one laughed at the understatement.

"Instead of stabbing Dougie in the heart, let's do this like we would in a real play and fake it. Go for his side. Aim the knife under his armpit. And Dougie. Sell it. Tchara, when you die, just make like you're having a seizure, so if we can't do a proper vanish ..."

"Got it," she said.

After we finished our best rehearsal in weeks, Kyle came up to me in the hall, apologized for joining the chorus of complaints and com-plimented me on getting everybody back on track. "I thought this was it. I thought everyone was going to quit. And I woulda gone with them. That was inspired."

"I can't believe it worked."

Kyle smiled. "Even in the most primitive of societies, man has always feared the psychopath."

If only the cigarette trick would work with the band. They still only had half the songs.

There was just one thing that still made me feel like this show might work, that we weren't going to play to empty houses and lose every cent we had and every cent we'd been able to borrow, that we'd pull a miracle out of our hats, because we had to. Cousin Jane. She was real and she believed and her faith reminded me that we weren't crazy. A professional promoter thought we were going to be the next big thing.

She went out with me one night to check how the band was doing. "They're great," she said. And she took my hand for a moment and held it. Then she asked how the show was coming together. I told her everything was on schedule. "Great," she said. "It's time to start lining up some press for you guys."

Press?

Cool. When we got back to the apartment, she showed me the release she'd sent out. Randy was at Bob's garage, working on the set.

I'd never seen a press release before. It was on pink paper and featured the Rainbow masthead and their logo—a pot of gold being guarded by a bad-assed leprechaun under a rainbow.

> *Rainbow Productions Ltd. is proud to present THE INITIATION, August 10–15 at the Robson Square Theatre. THE INITIATION is a new concept in theatre. It is a synthesis of magic, traditional drama, rock music, dance and mime.*

"Cool," I said.

> *The basic plot of THE INITIATION is the conflict between two beautiful sorceresses who are vying for the position of high priestess of the demonic arts. Their master is an evil villain known as Santar, who in the Darth Vader tradition is an evil incarnate.*

That didn't sound quite right, but it sounded impressive.

> *Once one of the sorceresses is chosen to be ordained as Santar's high priestess, she must undergo the rites of THE INITIATION. These rites include finding a victim whom she seduces, tortures and eventually kills.*
>
> *The people who put this show together are called Black Metal Fantasy Productions consisting of Mark Leiren-Young, a local science fiction writer ...*

Cool!

> *... and his colleague ...*

Randy was gonna hate this.

> *... Randy Kagna who has worked in the technical side of local theatre for years.*

Randy was really gonna hate this. It didn't even mention he was a magician.

> *The music is taped, but all original and played by Paranoia, who did the score for ANGST. The show runs at 8 pm every night except Saturday, which has two shows: 7 pm and 10 pm.*
>
> *THE INITIATION is completely funded through private individuals. Everyone in the show works as a volunteer with hope that any profits from this run will pay back some of the believing investors.*

Then it ended with the final line in bold capital letters:

> *BE THERE FOR A BRAND NEW KIND OF THEATRE EXPERIENCE.*

Wow. Randy would love this part. I did.

"Everybody in the media is gonna want to talk to you," said Jane.

Cousin Jane made it all feel real.

After Jane left, my brother came over to visit the apartment. He loved it, especially Randy's room with the blacklight posters and the waterbed. He was not impressed that I was sleeping on a couch. "One day you need a real bed," he said. Then he saw the handcuffs on the bong table and, before I could stop him, he tried them on. "These are so cool," he said as he snapped the second bracelet shut. "Where are the keys?"

"Randy doesn't have keys," I said.

"So how does he open them?" David asked in a slightly higher pitch.

"Magic," I said. And I started to laugh.

"Seriously," David asked, sounding both scared and angrier, "Where are the keys?" I kept laughing. David was not amused.

Fortunately, Randy was home early that night.

25

Almond Oil

Everybody wanted me to fire Tabitha. She'd known all her lines on the first day, but since that night in the car she never seemed to remember them. No matter what scene we were doing, Tabitha always looked like she was somewhere else—or wished she was. She barely acknowledged Annie and Ivy and once she was "in character" she'd only talk to Kyle. "I'm just being Tchara," she told me. "I'm supposed to be a bitch, right? Tchara would never acknowledge Santar's new girls."

She was right.

But Tchara was officially too bitchy for my two female leads.

And she was late again. Ivy was furious—and I hadn't seen Ivy get mad since Dougie's giggle fits. She was always the calmest person in the room, the one who just wanted to learn her lines and blocking and keep rolling. The one who would meet me during smoke breaks to ask about things like motivation. "She thinks she can get away with this superior act, just because she's your girlfriend."

"My what?"

Ivy looked more thrown than I did. "You mean she's not? No way."

Annie looked equally surprised. "We were sure that you two, you know."

"Uh, no," I said, wondering how they'd known about the night we'd made out in the car. I hadn't even told Dr. Bob. There was no way Tabitha told them, was there? And it had only happened once, much to my ever-growing frustration. "We're not," I said, hoping I wasn't blushing.

Not that I hadn't wished we were. But when I wasn't at rehearsals for the show, I was working with the band, or running errands to pick up pieces for the illusions, or trying to line up costumes, or meeting Jane about PR.

And Tabitha hadn't asked me to drive her again since that night. Since she was the least shy person I'd ever met, I figured that meant she didn't want me to.

"Then you've gotta talk to her," said Ivy. "You've gotta do something." She didn't say "or else," but it was hanging there in the auditorium's varnish-scented air.

When Tabitha showed up that evening and I said she was late, she just said she had missed her bus. "Do we have the illusion yet?"

"Soon," I said.

She gave me a look that said she believed this even less than I was starting to. She took her spot in the middle of our imaginary audience, then turned to me. "Ready when you are."

I wanted to say something snarky, but she looked really sexy and I was hoping we might make out again sometime, hopefully soon. Maybe that's why Ivy and Annie suspected something? We ran Tchara's scene a dozen times and she didn't seem remotely interested in it. During a smoke break, Kyle took me aside. "You have to cut her loose."

But ...

"She's not into it anymore. And she's really starting to piss Ivy off. If she keeps pulling this diva routine, you're gonna lose Ivy. And if we lose Ivy, we lose Annie. Those two are getting pretty tight."

We ran Tchara's scene again after the break and I knew Kyle was right. All the spark I'd seen in the auditions and our early rehearsals was gone. She hadn't been any good since ... the night I drove her home. Maybe I didn't have to fire her, but we had to talk or something, I was really hoping for "or something."

The band had a bar gig the next night. And Randy was working on the magic in Bob's garage every night till at least midnight. I suggested to Tabitha that maybe, if she didn't have anything else to do, she could come over to the apartment. To talk. She suggested maybe we could play Scrabble.

Scrabble. That would work. I was good at Scrabble.

We'd play Scrabble. We'd talk. We'd work things out.

When Tabitha showed up at the door she was dressed like Stevie Nicks.

I could see her bra through her white peasant blouse. I knew I wasn't supposed to look at her bra. Eye contact. Eyes. Be professional. Be nonchalant. At least be mature. And mature guys didn't stare at a girl's breasts, right? Eye contact. Jade green eyes. "Uh ... hi."

She walked into the apartment the same way she'd walked into the theatre that first day, the same way she'd walked into my car—like it was hers. She walked straight to the stereo to choose an album, flipping through my records like she knew what was there. "*Tusk*. I keep meaning to buy this," she said. "I love Stevie Nicks. Can I borrow it later?"

"Sure," I said.

She put side one of my new Fleetwood Mac double album on the turntable. Then she put her bag down. I hadn't noticed she was carrying a bag. "I brought some wine, too," she said.

Wine? "Great," I said, trying to sound like I had wine every night, or at least every night I had an actress over to discuss her performance.

"And some almond oil."

"I'm allergic to nuts," I said. If you'd given me a year I never would have guessed what the almond oil was for.

"It's for a massage," she said. "You don't have to lick it. Unless you want to."

So much for nonchalant. I was now completely chalant. I'd never been so chalant in my life. This was not a milk ad. "Wanna play Scrabble?" I asked, like the nerd I was.

"Sure," she said. "Let's play on the bed. This couch is a bed, right?"

We really did play Scrabble. At first. And our hands kept bumping into each other in the purple Chivas Regal bag when we reached for the letters. Then Tabitha played the word "fuck." It was on a double word score. "Forty-two points," she said.

"That's not legal," I said, achieving an all-new pinnacle of nerdiness. After all, slang wasn't allowed.

She didn't move her letters. "You look tense," she said. "I think you could use a massage."

I'd had a massage once. My Zayda Ben took me to a spa at the Harrison resort. Gus, an ancient bald guy with football-player muscles, pounded on my back until it felt like one giant bruise.

"I'm really good," she purred. "Take your shirt off."

"Take my what?"

"C'mon," she said. "It's no big deal. Just a massage."

I stood up, took off my shirt and she opened my couch bed. "You need to be able to lie down," she said. Before I could reply she said, "So lie down." And I did.

Then she reached into her purse. The moment I felt her warm hands touch my back, I knew this wasn't going to be anything like my experience with Gus. I felt something moist trickling down my back. "This is the almond oil," she said. Her fingers dug into my shoulders. "Relax," she said. "I won't bite. At least not till later."

As her fingers slowly made their way down the side of my back, it was already the most erotic experience I'd ever had. Her palms pressed into my back and then she got up on the bed, so she was straddling me. "This'll make it easier," she said. Then she lowered herself onto me, sitting on my butt. "More pressure this way," she said. Yes, pressure. I was definitely feeling more pressure. Good pressure. Yay pressure.

"My turn," she said eventually. And she may have had to say it twice, since I'd left the planet. I had no idea how long I'd been in my trance, but I snapped out of it completely when I looked up and realized she'd taken off her shirt and was starting to unsnap her bra. "This'll make it easier," she said.

"Sure," I squeaked, as she handed me the bottle of oil.

Then she lay down on the bed. I was kneeling beside her as I squirted the first bit of oil onto her back. "Pressure," she said.

I tried to move into the same position she'd been in, without letting her know how much I was enjoying myself. I started to press my palms into her back. "Harder," she whispered. "I'm not fragile." I pressed harder and she started to moan. I'd never heard a moan like that. I stopped for a moment to shift myself, suddenly aware of how close my crotch was to her jeans. As I was about to pull back, she flipped over.

"Don't stop," she said."

I didn't stop, I froze. "I just. Uh. Where do you ..."

"Don't you like them?" she asked.

This couldn't be happening. I managed to mutter a "Yeah."

"You should massage them, too," she said. "Use some oil."

So I did.

"They won't break," she said. And she let loose that moan again, except this time it was deeper, longer. "Yeah," she said. "Like that."

"Like that," I agreed.

"That's good," she said.

"Good," I said. At least I think I said something. I may have just kept massaging. I could have kept massaging all night.

"We should take a bath," she said.

I know I *thought* words, but as she unsnapped her jeans and slid them off in front of me, none came out. I was still watching that scene in my head when she disappeared into the bathroom and turned on the water. This was definitely a signal.

I went to Randy's bedroom and searched for something I never thought I'd need. Actually, I searched for two things I never thought

I'd need. I took a coat hanger out of his closet—and a condom out of his bedside table.

"I'm waiting," she said. And she was.

"I added some bubble bath," she said. Bubbles. Yes, there were bubbles. But not enough to hide her breasts. "Get in. It's big enough for both of us."

Only if we sat very close together …

"Come on. We don't want the water to get cold."

I approached the tub and was about to step in.

"Take off your underwear," she said.

Right, that made sense. I'd never been naked with a girl in the room before, but taking off the rest of my clothes before getting into a tub made sense.

After much mutual soaping we helped each other dry off before Tabitha took my hand and led me back to my couch. We weren't that dry. We also weren't dressed.

She spotted the condom I'd placed on the bedside table and stared at it a moment. I felt like an idiot. I'd assumed that just because we were naked it meant that we might, just might, possibly, maybe …

"You don't need to worry about birth control."

That wasn't quite the response I'd started bracing for.

"I still have my diaphragm in."

I wasn't sure exactly what a diaphragm was, but I knew what it was for. It was the word "still" that threw me.

"I fucked this guy yesterday."

She … what?

I didn't want to think about this. We'd just had a massage and a bath and now she was letting me know she already had birth control in place and for some reason I still couldn't stop my lips from moving. "You have a boyfriend?

"Not exactly," she said as she pulled me down on the couch toward her. "Friend of my dad's. A professor."

Friend of her dad's? I tried to shake the image. And when she pulled my hands to her breasts I had pretty much succeeded until, "I've never done it with anybody who's practically my own age before."

Something about this seemed even more dangerous than having sex with Annie. I wanted her to stop talking. More than anything else I'd ever wanted in the world I wanted her to stop talking. I definitely didn't want her to say, "I think the youngest guy I ever did before was in his thirties."

I couldn't think about this. And I couldn't stop myself from asking, "And this professor ..."

She rolled toward me. "Don't worry. Your cock is way bigger than his."

There were a thousand questions that had popped into my head that I was trying to ignore. That was not one of them. I said, "Thanks," but even if that had been true, her compliment no longer applied.

"What's wrong?"

"Nothing," I said. But suddenly this felt all wrong. She'd probably said everything a friend of her father's would have wanted to hear, maybe needed to hear in order to feel good about what he was doing with a sixteen-year-old girl—and nothing nothing nothing at all that a not-quite eighteen-year-old who'd never been this close to a naked girl before could remotely cope with.

"I never like guys my own age, but this is the perfect start to my theatre career, right. Fucking the director?" Then she laughed. I didn't.

"Come on," she said. "It's funny." Then she did her best Marilyn voice, "Now can I get a bigger part, Mr. Director?"

For the first time in months I'd forgotten about the play. And I'd completely forgotten I was supposed to fire her, or at least adjust her attitude.

"I can't," I said.

"Can't?" She said it like she'd never heard the word before. Then ... "You're not gay, are you?"

Before I could say anything, she moved a hand to check. "No," she said. "Definitely not gay. So what's wrong?"

What was wrong was the idea of her having sex with her father's friends and knowing she still had a diaphragm in place from the professor she'd been with yesterday, knowing I was about to do something completely unethical and ...

"Oh my God. You're a virgin."

That too.

I must have blushed, because a moment later she shrieked with laughter. "That's so ... *cute*."

"Cute" was a bigger mood killer than dubious older lovers and my ethics problem. "This'll be great. I always wanted to do a virgin." A moment later her head disappeared under my sheets, she was doing something I'd only ever read about in Randy's magazines and all thoughts of right and wrong vanished. Suddenly, too suddenly, Tabitha's head reappeared. "Ever had a girl do that before?"

I didn't speak. I couldn't speak. I didn't have to.

"Didn't think so," she said. "Let's fuck. And then I'll do it again."

I wanted to protest. I knew I shouldn't do this. It was wrong. I might be firing her and as she started talking to me using lines I'd only read in Randy's magazines, there was something about what she was saying, how she was saying it, that made it seem like I wasn't the person she was there with. And the closer I got to her, the dirtier she started talking—and the dirtier she talked, the more it reminded me that I had no clue what I was doing. It was wrong and I knew it and I couldn't say anything, because I couldn't speak, couldn't breathe and couldn't think. "Right here," she said.

And I was about to go right there when we heard the key in the lock. It was Randy. The only time I'd ever put out the coat hanger and the selfish bastard ignored it.

Tabitha pulled the sheet over her face so fast we could have worked it into the show as a disappearance and as the door swung open she hissed the same way I'd imagined her hissing as Tchara. "Tell him to get the hell out."

I jumped off the bed, grabbed a towel to cover myself and ran to the door. Randy was standing there, looking startled, spaced out. "Coat hanger," I snarled.

"Coat hanger? Did I forget to take it down? Sorry, man. Long night."

That was when he looked at me and realized ...

"It's mine."

"Whoa," said Randy.

I was wearing a towel. And I wasn't wearing it, just holding it strategically.

"You have company?" He sounded shocked, but impressed. He spotted Tabitha's top on the floor outside the bathroom. "No way. You and Ms. T!"

He lowered his voice to a whisper. "Brushing up on her lines?"

I could have begged him to leave. I could have told him to leave. I could have punched him in the stomach and let him die in the hall while I got laid. But I didn't. I couldn't explain why—even to myself—but I knew it was the right thing to do. And I despised myself for doing it.

By the time I got back to the living room, Tabitha was dressed and she'd folded the bed back into a couch. She didn't say anything until we got into the car. "I wasn't gonna fuck with an audience in the next room," she said with a fury that would have terrified Santar, maybe even Shawn.

I tried to find the right words. "Maybe it's better we didn't," I said.

"Better?"

Wrong words. Definitely the wrong words.

"Better?"

"I mean we are working together."

She looked steamed—and you can take that as many ways as you like. I kept driving, kept my eyes on the road. "You should've kicked him out."

"It's his place," I said.

"So couldn't he have gone to Denny's or something?"

"It's uh ..."

"It's the milk ad girl thing, isn't it?"

"No. It's like ... more like ... you're like a friend and ..."

Another wrong answer. "A friend? I don't blow my friends."

"I'm sorry, I mean ..." I didn't know what I meant. I didn't even know what "blow" meant.

"You'll regret this," she said. "You're always going to regret this. For as long as you live."

"No," I said in my best Clint Eastwood monotone. "You will." She got out of the car like she'd paid me to drive her home and didn't even bother to slam the door, just stormed out, leaving it open for me to shut myself. I knew I'd never see my *Tusk* album again.

And I never did.

26

Paradise by the Dashboard Lights

You will? She'd regret it? What the hell was I talking about? I was a seventeen-year-old virgin, a few weeks away from being an eighteen-year-old virgin. I'd practically kicked a naked girl out of my bed, a live naked girl who wanted to have sex with me. I should have wanted to kill Randy, but part of me—definitely not my groin—felt like I'd been rescued.

When I got back home, Randy was on my couch watching the *Star Trek* episode where Kirk made out with the green-skinned alien babe. I had to tell him what happened. I had to tell someone what happened and at 2 a.m. my choices were Randy or the waitress at Denny's. I told him everything. Okay, almost everything.

"You should be proud of yourself," he said. "You did the right thing. How would you have felt if you had sex with her and then fired her tomorrow?"

I had no idea how I would have felt—*because I was a virgin.* Maybe I would have felt like a guy who'd had sex. "So you wouldn't have slept with her?"

Randy laughed. "Of course I would have."

Of course he would have.

183

"But you're a lot nicer than I am."

I couldn't believe we'd finally lost a cast member because of sex and it wasn't Randy's fault. Although if he hadn't unlocked that door, I probably would have let the rest of the cast go before firing the first girl I'd ever had sex with.

When the cast heard Tabitha was gone, there wasn't much mourning.

"Maybe Tina could play Tchara," chirped Annie. Yes, perfect, things were going so well that we were going to bring in her scary sister to save the day.

"I've got someone in mind," I lied. Then I had them run a scene while I tried to figure out who that someone would be. I'd never imagined replacing Tabitha, never imagined anyone else in the part. Tabitha was Tchara.

I knew I could call one of the other actresses we'd auditioned but … with the show opening in less than three weeks and a magic show that still had no magic in it … would they still want to get involved? Would anyone who saw how unprepared we were want to get involved?

That night I drove to Lisa Jorgensen's house and begged her to take some time off from her job at Young Ms. When she agreed I felt like we could do anything and that maybe this was what it would take to kick Randy into high gear.

When I told him the news he was thrilled and promised everything was almost ready. "Let's go to Denny's to celebrate," he said.

"We'll celebrate the first time we kill Dougie onstage," I said.

Then Jane called. She wanted to come over to the apartment. She had something to tell us. I figured she'd lined up some interviews, maybe some TV.

"They're sending me out on tour. With *Beatlemania*. I'm going to Calgary with the show tomorrow." Jane was excited. "This is a big break for me, a big responsibility."

I felt sick. It wasn't possible.

"You can't." said Randy. "How will you survive without me?"

I was more concerned with how we'd survive without her.

"I'll be in touch," said Jane, almost flirting back. "Don't worry, guys, I asked Brad to look after the show personally. I gave him your poster concept, the media list, the marketing plan, everything. You'll be great."

"When do we see the poster?"

"Soon," she said.

"So we're not doing a photo shoot?" asked Randy. "I thought we'd have photos of Annie and Ivy. And me."

"Too expensive," said Jane.

I tried to tell myself this would be good for the show. Brad was the best. He had to be, didn't he? How else would a show about the Beatles be selling out?

"I promise I'll be back in time for opening. Before we take you out on tour."

It had been a while since anyone had talked about the tour. Just hearing the word again reminded us how big this was, how big this could be, why Brad Bowen—the bow in Rainbow—was promoting us. We were going to tour the world.

"I wish I could see a rehearsal before I go. I'm really excited about seeing all that magic."

Me too, I thought.

"Wanna see some now?" asked Randy. He brought out a bag of lemons and asked Jane for a dollar bill.

After Jane produced the money she told us both not to worry. "It'll be great. Brad's the best."

Then Randy had her choose a lemon and did a trick where he sliced her dollar out of the fruit. Jane was impressed. I was depressed.

The day after Jane left, it got worse.

I could handle actors who couldn't always act. I could handle the magician who hadn't delivered our magic. It was the band that almost killed me.

They'd finished the songs and had started at the recording studio in Surrey. So now every afternoon I'd run errands until six, rehearse until ten, then spend sixty minutes driving across two bridges and along some nasty stretches of highway to get to a garage with a machine that recorded sixteen tracks for forty dollars an hour.

Elmer, the guy who ran the studio, wore a cowboy hat and talked with a Nashville drawl even though I suspect the deepest south he'd been was touring with his country band around Seattle. Elmer's garage was decorated with the cardboard covers of albums he'd mixed and a few albums he'd performed on. Elmer was a country guitar player and he mostly recorded country music. So the first time he said he didn't like the sound of our band, I figured it was 'cause no one was singin' about hurtin' or cheatin' or trucks. I didn't say that, I just shrugged. But he knew what I meant. "I've recorded metal," he said. "I've recorded songs that would make your ears bleed. I just don't think these guys have their act together."

This threw me.

"Songs aren't bad. Lyrics are kinda clever, if you like that sort of pretentious Pink Floydy thing but ..." I waited for his next move. "They're just not that tight. It's like they just wrote these songs."

"They did," I said.

"You should toss these guys now and get studio musicians in here."

I'd never heard of studio musicians. "They only did this so they could get studio experience," I said. "That's our deal."

The music stopped again. Elmer clicked on his microphone to talk to the band—they were behind a plastic window surrounded by their instruments and a collection of strategically placed microphones. "What is it this time?"

Gord, the bass player, piped up, "Think I came in late."

"Go again," said Elmer. And they did.

"*Sgt. Pepper* didn't have this many takes."

"They just wanna get it right," I suggested hopefully.

"You can't afford to wait till they get it right," said Elmer. "I tried to get them to record their parts separately, but they're set on being live from the floor."

As if on cue, they stopped again. This time it was harmonies. "I came in early," said Rafe.

Elmer nodded, signalled for them to go again, then muttered the suggestion one more time. "Studio musicians," he said. "Or these guys are gonna cost you a fortune."

One night Dr. Bob asked if he could come with me to see what a studio session was like. After the band spent three hours not recording *Voices*, I drove home and was so tired I shut my eyes on the Pattullo Bridge. I was heading straight for the railing when Bob screamed and woke me up. Like I said, it was the band that almost killed me.

When I got home there was a message on the answering machine to pick up the posters. Randy's job was downtown, so I asked him to pick them up after work. I told him to bring them to the JCC for rehearsal. If we didn't have magic yet I needed something to boost morale and remind everyone this was real.

When Randy didn't show up I didn't care how many coat hangers were on the door, I was going in and I was gonna kill him. The cast had spent the whole night begging me to show them the posters. They were more excited about the posters than the magic.

There weren't any coat hangers on the door. And when I walked in, before I could ask where the hell he'd been, the first words out of Randy's mouth were, "I'm so sorry."

"Where were you?" I asked.

"I couldn't," he said. "I didn't think I should." He looked like Heidi had after the call about her mom's heart attack.

"Are you okay?"

He lifted a shiny square of white paper a little larger than an album cover and held it up long enough so I could stare at it until my heart broke.

I'm sure Jane had told the artists at Rainbow to do something great with the picture, but instead ...

There was a black silhouette of Santar in his Viking helmet—at least we assumed it was Santar because he was wearing a pentagram on his chest. On either side of him were James Bond type silhouettes standing in flames, just like we'd suggested, just like Kyle sketched. Their breasts were absurd even by *Heavy Metal* standards and wherever they were posing it was obviously really, really, really cold, despite being surrounded by flames. But the pièce de résistance was Santar's sword. At least we hoped it was Santar's sword. Freud would have blushed.

We would have been better off photocopying Kyle's napkin.

But that wasn't the worst part.

"Five bucks," said Randy.

I don't think Randy had noticed Santar looked like a porn star. And I hadn't noticed the line beneath the ridiculous image that he'd fixated on: "Advance tickets five dollars."

No. It couldn't be. "How are we supposed to make any money if our tickets are only five dollars?"

We'd never talked about prices with Rainbow. They were the experts, so we'd just assumed ...

"We have to sell two thousand tickets just to break even."

As bad as I was at math, I'd already come up with the same terrifying numbers. Six shows. One hundred and ninety-eight seats. Even I could do the math to realize that ten thousand divided by five equalled ...

"We are so screwed." Randy had already finished the calculations.

27

Hell's Gate

"**C**an you swim?" The studly surfer dude was handing me my life vest and a clipboard with a release form.

Of course I could swim. I'd taken lessons as a kid at the JCC. I could ... Well, I could float anyway.

Surfer dude was leading the "whitewater rafting adventure" Bob had dragged me on, and he told us we all had to sign a waiver confirming we could swim that released the company from any liability in the event we fell into the water and didn't swim well enough to survive in the rapids. "We haven't lost anybody yet," he said with the serious expression he'd obviously practised to scare the rubes, "but it happens. That's why our company only hires team captains with lifeguard certification." I expected him to flex. After all, he wasn't just a guy with a big paddle, a shiny orange life vest and a serious tan, he was a "team captain." He flashed his perfect teeth instead. The eight trainee nurses from Bob's dad's hospital all looked like they were making plans to fall into the water in the hopes of needing mouth-to-mouth.

I couldn't believe I was here. I had a show opening in less than two weeks—a magic show that had no magic tricks. How could I take two days off?

"It'll be fun." Bob had repeated this since the day he'd first told me to sign up. I didn't get the appeal. We were paying a hundred bucks each to hop in a big rubber dinghy and set off through a stretch of water that the pioneers who had no choice but to take this trip a hundred years earlier if they wanted to get to Vancouver had unironically named "Hell's Gate." And why were we doing this? A quick adrenalin rush? I'd had no lack of adrenalin hits lately. But Bob kept telling me it would be a great way for me to take my mind off the show.

Yeah. That was going to happen. The set wasn't ready, the magic wasn't finished, the band had only recorded half the songs and we'd only sold two dozen advance tickets—and those included the six I'd sold to my parents and the three Bob had sold to his parents and sister. The only way I was forgetting the show now was if I was lucky enough to fly out of the raft and crush my skull on the rocks.

If Bob hadn't been building the set—in his dad's garage—and hadn't told me that if I cancelled on him, we'd have to find a new building space, I would have bailed. I didn't need a vacation. I needed a miracle.

But since Bob had first told me about this trip, he'd been obsessed by it. By the time we got in the van with his friends from the hospital, he was an expert on Hell's Gate. He was telling me all about the canyon and the type of rafts and the company and ...

He was looking right past me at the redheaded nursing student from Montreal. Cecile. This wasn't about rafting or helping me forget the show. I was the decoy, his wingman. Cecile was going on the trip with all her friends from work. Bob was younger than the other guys at work, he was a jock in a universe of geeks and, strike three, his dad was the boss—so all the other guys kept their distance. That meant Bob had a choice. He could go on the trip solo and look like a loser or ... "Mark's never been rafting," he announced to Cecile's ultra-blonde friend, Christina. "He really wanted to do this."

Cecile was cute—but old. At least as old as Jane. Normally when I was out with Bob I forgot he was almost twenty. But now, surrounded by Bob's co-workers and seeing the way Cecile was smiling back at him, I remembered he really was two years and change older than me. After feeling like an adult since the moment I'd moved in with Randy, I felt like a kid. And that was before we got to the campsite when Cecile asked if I was Bob's little brother and he hesitated before answering.

Bob and I spent most of the afternoon trying to set up our tent. There were metal sticks and lots of plastic pegs and an instruction guide and the more we moved these things around and tried to get them to connect, the more I understood the appeal of sleeping under the trees. Or drowning. Finally, after I stopped "helping," Bob managed to put all the pieces together to resemble something that looked sort of like the diagram in the manual. I went for a walk and stared at the water while Bob went back to the main campsite and stared at Cecile. It really was quiet and, as I sat there surrounded by nature, all I could think about was ... how the band was burning up studio time and money we didn't have playing take 666 of *Lead me to Lucifer*.

Dinner was camp food—hot dogs, hamburgers, marshmallows— and afterwards, one of the doctors, or nurses, or interns started passing a joint. When it reached me, I stared at it and then ... instead of passing it, I moved it toward my mouth and ...

Dr. Bob grabbed it and passed it to Cecile. "You don't do drugs," said Bob.

"Maybe that's a mistake," I said.

Cecile started handing it back, but Dr. Bob stopped her. "It's okay," he said. "He doesn't smoke." She shrugged. Actually, she did that thing French people do that's like a shrug but subtler and sexier, and passed the joint to Christina.

Bob led me away, into a clearing. "If you wanna get high some time, fine, but not tonight." Tonight seemed like a perfect night to me. My life was falling apart. We were unlikely to get busted by cops in the middle of a forest. And if anything was wrong with the drugs, I was surrounded by medical professionals.

Bob disagreed. "Drugs will intensify whatever you're feeling. I don't think you need that tonight."

I'd thought drugs made you forget what you were feeling and made you happy, or mellow, or stupid. Any of the above would have been fantastic. But if drugs would just make me feel like more of a loser, they probably weren't a great idea.

I'd promised myself I wouldn't ask Bob about the show—but I hadn't promised Bob. And I was starting to realize I'd lied to myself about a lot of things. He'd been up all night the night before building. I had to know how the levitation was coming along. He looked like I'd spoken to him in tongues. I definitely didn't want this feeling intensified, this very sick feeling.

Bob didn't know about the levitation, or the table for stabbing Dougie, or the tube for stabbing Dougie, or the sceptre of the solid flame. He just knew what he'd seen in his garage, where all the props were being built—the one part of the show I hadn't paid any attention to because it required two things I didn't understand: tools and blueprints. Aside from not knowing how things were built, I had no idea how much they cost and never thought about where we were getting our supplies.

As we stood in the forest, Dr. Bob told me Randy, David and Randy's friend George—who had a pickup—had become experts at "finding" wood for the sets and props.

"Where do you find wood?"

"Construction sites. Whenever we run out of lumber, they get in George's pickup, drive to a site and then they have David toss a ball into the yard and chase it. If there's no security guards or dogs they ... find some wood."

Randy was stealing wood?

My little brother was stealing wood?

I'd assumed the late-night building sessions were about getting things done after Randy finished at the office, not because it was easier to "acquire" supplies in the dark. Bob told me he wouldn't help

Randy acquire supplies. "I'm already in enough trouble with my dad for taking over the garage." And he still wants to know why he had to buy tickets to the show when it's being built in his garage with his tools.

"Please tell me the tricks are done."

Bob looked at me apologetically. "I thought you were buying tricks."

"If you're not building tricks what are you working on?"

"Satan," said Bob.

I could wait for Satan. I could live without Satan. But I needed the fire pond. I needed the levitation, I needed a way to kill Dougie and the more Bob talked the more I thought I needed a way to kill Randy, too.

"It's almost done," he said. "It's pretty cool."

Almost done was good. "That's great," I said. And he thought it was cool. Cool. "So it's actually scary?"

If only Satan would scare me half as much as the shocked look on Bob's face ... "It's supposed to be scary? He didn't say it was supposed to be scary."

I hoped Bob was kidding. I prayed he was kidding. "Of course it's supposed to be scary. It's supposed to be as scary as the thing that jumps out of the guy's chest in *Alien*." That's when Bob started to laugh.

"What does it look like?"

Bob couldn't stop laughing, but he managed to get a few words out. What I thought I heard through his snorfling noises were the terrifying words, "Miss Piggy with horns."

Bob walked back to camp. I didn't. I sat under a tree, stared at the stars and realized I was no longer remotely scared of the whitewater. Considering Satan was killing me, what could be more appropriate than facing death at Hell's Gate?

The whitewater was breathtaking in the true sense of the word— the same basic effect as riding a roller coaster, but with the bonus terror of knowing there's no safety bar or emergency brake. The best part was when we hit a calm pool and a few of the people in our raft got into a splash fight with a few people in the other raft and I got to soak some snarky doctors-in-training before the raft tipped and Bob and I ended up finding out how well the life preservers worked.

I didn't forget about *The Initiation* for the whole trip, but I forgot about it for the three hours we were on the raft. And I treasured those hours, because the moment we stepped off the raft I started to picture Muppet Satan again and wanted to scream, or cry, or help Shawn pulverize Randy.

I held it together on the drive back to the city. I held it together while Bob said goodbye to Cecile. And then we got in my Honda Civic and drove about six blocks before I finally started to cry. Bob must have seen nervous breakdowns before, because he was completely calm—or maybe things had gone better with Cecile than I'd thought? "It'll be fine," he said.

"No," I said. I knew it wouldn't. I couldn't say it out loud to anyone else involved with the show because they'd make a run for it and then things would get even worse, but I had to admit it. I pulled into a parking lot across the street from our old high school.

"No. It's gonna be a disaster. We're doing a magic show and the best trick we've got is Ivy miming like she's caught in a box. And she's a lousy mime. The band thinks they're making *Dark Side of the Moon*. Annie can't kiss Kyle or her boyfriend will kill us all. And that's if Annie's boyfriend doesn't kill Randy for making out with his girlfriend. Tabitha quit. Our only illusion is Muppet Satan. No one's going to show up. And we're gonna owe my uncle ten thousand bucks."

"You borrowed ten thousand bucks? Ten thousand bucks? To do this? Are you out of your mind?"

I forgot I hadn't told him that part.

"I thought this was Randy's money you were losing. Are you nuts?!"

The money was bad, but there was something worse, something I couldn't even admit to Bob above a whisper. "The worst part ... I don't even want anyone to see the thing because it's gonna be the worst show in the history of theatre." I'd said it and I felt ... like committing ritual suicide. "But if no one sees the thing I lose even more money."

I started to cry again.

"The floor looks great," said Bob.

I was still crying, but now I was laughing, too. "If we can just get the audience to stare at the floor for the whole show we're golden."

Bob laughed. "And the walls—the walls are fantastic."

We were so screwed.

"So what do you wanna do?" Bob asked,

"Nothing I can do. Like on the stupid raft. Just hang on and hope we don't die."

Then Bob made a suggestion no theatre person would ever make, a suggestion no theatre person would have considered. But Bob wasn't a theatre person—he was a scientist who was helping out with the set because, for some inexplicable reason, he thought I was worth putting up with. "Can't you just cancel the show?"

I couldn't believe what he'd said. Cancel the show? This was sacrilege. It was madness. "You can't cancel a show. The show must go on."

"Why?"

I couldn't believe he was asking this. I also couldn't come up with an answer.

Dr. Bob examined me like I was a scientific anomaly. "So ... I dunno ... why can't you just ... I dunno ... wait till it's ready?"

"Will those tricks ever be ready?"

"No."

Not the answer I was expecting. "Why not?"

"I don't think Randy knows how to build them."

I'd lost my soul to Muppet Satan. I knew it. I didn't want to admit it, but I knew it. I'd known it for a few weeks now. We would have been better off buying our tricks at Jacko's. When I got back to the apartment I asked Randy if the illusions were ready. He didn't make eye contact. "Almost," he said.

I stared at him. "But they'll be ready for Friday?"

"No problem," said Randy. "The show must go on."

Says who?

The next morning, I made some calls.

28

Birthday Presence

"We're here to see Brad Bowen." The receptionist, a wiry Joey Ramone wannabe in his early twenties, didn't even look up at me and Dr. Bob as we crowded his desk. I hoped that if Dr. Bob was with me that just maybe I'd have enough nerve to do this. "You got an appointment?"

"I'm writing *The Initiation*."

"The what?"

"This," I said. I put one of our tacky handbills on his desk. Joey scowled at it like it was diseased. "Brad's busy," he said. "You can make an appointment."

Brad was in his office. Behind Joey. Brad wasn't even on the phone. I looked at Bob, Bob looked at me, Bob looked back at the desk dweeb. "Thanks, we'll see ourselves in."

Joey sputtered, Brad looked up at Bob and me, assessed our threat level, like maybe he had a gun in his drawer and was deciding whether to reach for it. He waved Joey out of the office.

"You're that kid," he said to me. "With Jane's little magic show."

"*The Initiation*," I said.

"Right," he said. "How's that going anyway?" Why couldn't he play Satan?

"Not so well," I said.

"Too bad," he said. "Too bad. What can I do for you?"

I had a speech prepared. I'd practised it in the car. Bob had heard the speech. He'd been impressed. I couldn't remember any of it.

"We want to get out of our deal."

I'd figured he'd yell. I thought there was a good chance he'd call in a team of bouncers and toss us through his third-storey window onto Cambie Street. I never would have guessed he'd just look back at me like I was kidding. "Come on, what do you really want?"

"You haven't done a thing for us."

"We did the posters and the press release and got you a theatre. We put ads in the papers. I'm sorry if this wasn't what you expected, but we've done our job."

Now I remembered my speech. "The posters are shit. The deal with the theatre is ridiculous. I'll bet you didn't even negotiate our rate. I know you didn't get us your special ad rate for the papers. I checked." And I had. That morning. "You haven't done anything for us since you sent Jane to Calgary. We're opening in nine days and nobody even answers our calls at your office. No one in your office seems to know our show exists. That guy doesn't and he answers your phones."

Brad wasn't smiling anymore. "Do you know anything about contracts?"

"A bit," I said.

"We have one," said Brad. "I suggest you read it. Now get out."

"I did read it. It says we get to approve the art and the ads."

"You get to consult."

"They suck."

"Consider yourself consulted." And he waved me away.

But I wasn't leaving. I couldn't leave. Not yet. "Jane said you'd put up the posters. And I haven't seen any out there. Nowhere."

"We'll put yours up next time we have a poster run. We can't do a special run for your show. I'm sure we've got a poster run soon."

"We're opening in nine days."

"Jane wants to do this theatre thing, that's fine. Hey, I hope you're a big hit. But my business is concerts."

The phone rang. Brad grabbed it, started barking orders, talking numbers and waved us away. He wanted me to disappear, but I didn't. When he hung up I was still there. "Look, kid, this is cute and everything, but I've got work to do."

"You're fired," I said.

It may have been the funniest thing he'd ever heard. He looked at me like this was the funniest thing he'd ever heard. But he didn't laugh. I think he was already turning this into an anecdote he'd tell his buddies over drinks. "You signed a contract."

"Yeah, I did," I said. "But I'm pretty sure it's not legal to sign a contract with someone who's only seventeen."

This seemed to startle him, but only for a moment. "So what? I've seen the other guy, the magician. He's what. Twenty?"

"Nineteen," I said.

"So he's legal," Brad looked ready to push the eject button to send us flying out the window.

"That's why I didn't let him sign. I'm eighteen in September," I said. "And I signed everything."

"But the deal is with the magician."

"No, the deal is with Black Metal Fantasy Productions. I'm the secretary, so I signed."

"But a seventeen-year-old can't sign for a company."

"I didn't think so," I said. "But if you still want to sue me, go for it. Maybe if you're lucky you'll win my whole comic collection."

He looked like the devil, I felt like one. It was the kind of perfect moment that usually only happens in the movies and I felt like making a movie just to immortalize it because …

That's when Brad's head exploded—bits of brain and shattered skull flew everywhere, just like in Cronenberg's *Scanners*.

"We'll pay you for the ads," I said, trying to sound reasonable, like

I was doing him a favour. "Just the printing costs. That's it. I'm not paying a cent for the shitty design. Or this shitty poster. Or these shitty handbills." Now that I'd started swearing I was getting the hang of it. "We're not paying you 30 percent for making this into a disaster."

"Seventeen," he said flatly. "Big brass ones for seventeen."

"Wanna see my driver's licence?" And even though I was sure he was going to lunge across his desk and strangle me, I smiled. "My birthday's September fourth."

Then Brad Bowen reminded himself that he was Brad Bowen and I was just a kid. He reminded himself the show was going to be a disaster and no matter how much he wanted to crush me, 30 percent of nothing wasn't worth a call to his lawyer. "I never wanted anything to do with this show anyway. Just make sure you take our name off the ads."

"Thank you," I said.

He did not say, "You're welcome."

I moved quickly, before he could tell me I had to take Rainbow's name off the posters, too. I had no intention of doing that. The posters looked ugly enough without having to cross out the Rainbow logo. Besides, I was still hoping his name would sell some tickets. Just because he was no longer promoting our show didn't mean I had to tell anyone he was no longer promoting our show.

When we got in the elevator, Bob stared at me like I was an alien. "You were great in there." And even though my legs were trembling so badly I could barely stand, I started to laugh.

Bob laughed too.

Our next stop was the Waterfront Theatre.

I'd called every theatre in town and the only one with an opening in the next two months was the Waterfront. It had just under three hundred seats, a good stage for magic, plenty of wing space and, best of all, the rental rates were less than half what Rainbow had "negotiated" as our price for Robson Square.

That's how I knew Brad hadn't shopped around for us. I'd found better rates in two hours. And unlike Robson Square, the Waterfront didn't take ten percent of the door as a "service charge."

The hard part as Bob and I sat across from the Waterfront manager in his tiny office was explaining why we wanted a new theatre and a new opening date for a show that was scheduled to open in nine days

We're not ready. We haven't sold any tickets. We suck ... No, that wasn't going to work at all. "There's an illness in the cast," I said. "One of our leads."

"Can't you just replace them? The show must go on and all that." The manager was very polite, very British and very sincere.

"It's not a regular show," I explained. "It's magic. We can't just teach anyone the secrets."

"Oh," he said. "I understand."

And I think he did.

"I'm sure we can work something out."

"That's great," I said.

"And Robson Square's all right with this then?"

"Absolutely," I lied.

"Very well then. I'll have the papers ready for you tomorrow."

"Perfect," I said. And for the first time since riding the rapids, I felt like I could breathe again. We were going to postpone the show. We were going to open in a month, in a real theatre. We'd have time to rehearse the tricks we had, replace the tricks we didn't, integrate the soundtrack and switch out any songs the band hadn't recorded with songs from Styx. And we'd be opening in September, which meant we could advertise at all the high schools to help scare up an audience. We could also double our ticket prices.

I knew the cast would be furious. Some of them might even quit. All of them might quit. But I didn't care. If Kyle left, I'd replace him with Randy. At least he'd wear the stupid helmet. If Dougie left I could be the victim. I could use an excuse to scream every night. If one of the girls left I could beg Tabitha to come back—maybe kiss and make up. Maybe make up and do a lot more than just kiss. Maybe the show wouldn't be a disaster after all. With this new theatre and with Rainbow out of the picture we might even make money.

When we got into the car, Bob said he had no idea I could lie like that. I told him it was news to me, too. "Randy's gonna be pretty happy you pulled this off."

"I hope so," I said.

Now Bob looked even more impressed. "You haven't told him yet?"

29

The Gorgon

"You did what!!!!!!!!!!"

Like I said, I'm not a big fan of exclamation marks, but Randy was so angry I could see the cartoon balloon over his head. He used a lot of exclamation marks along with all the symbols for cartoon swearing. I'd taken him for a walk to the beach, told him I had great news. This was like proposing, it had to be done properly.

"What did Rainbow say?"

The look on Randy's face when I told him I'd fired Rainbow was even funnier than the look on Brad Bowen's. "You what?" He used up another romance fiction novel's worth of exclamation marks and a year's supply of question marks.

"It's gonna be great," I said. "All I have to do is get us out of the deal with Robson Square and it's done. The Waterfront is perfect."

"I can't believe you did this without talking to me."

"I can't believe we open in nine days and we still don't know how we're supposed to kill Dougie onstage. And we don't have any tricks ready yet. None."

"I've got the tube for the sword to kill Dougie. "

"Do you have the sword?"

Randy looked at the sand.

"If we open in a few days this is gonna be a joke. Do you want anyone to see this?"

He didn't say anything. He didn't have to.

"Do any of your tricks work yet?"

Somehow he had the gall to look outraged instead of embarrassed. "Satan's really cool."

"You tell me what magic tricks you can have ready and I'll rewrite the show around them. I don't care if it's cups and balls, vanishing scarves and the dove pan. The stuff we did at the JCC was way better than this, so let's just do the stuff we did at the JCC if we have to."

"The actors will quit."

"So?"

I could see him thinking about it. "We just go with the magic we've got?" The exclamation marks had vanished along with the outrage. He was starting to smile. It had been weeks since I'd seen him smile.

"This is supposed to be a magic show. Let's go with magic that works. Since we're not gonna be touring we can even use the old music. Pull the plug on the soundtrack before the band wastes any more studio time. Cut our losses."

The smile was growing. "If we postpone this, can I do a few more tricks? Maybe something with Lisa?"

"No problem," I said.

"What do we tell the cast?"

"We blame Rainbow. Tell them they screwed up. I mean, they did, right?"

Randy nodded. "We blame Rainbow ... I love it."

He reached for a joint, looked at it, then put it back in his pocket. "What went wrong?"

I knew this was the type of thing we were supposed to be able to laugh about one day, hopefully on *The Tonight Show*, but that day wasn't going to arrive for a long time. "Everything."

"If I was onstage ..."

"Yeah."

"I never wanted to be a techie. I wanted to be onstage and then ... It's my show and I'm barely even onstage except for the opening and closing. I'm the magician."

For the first time in months I felt sorry for Randy. And I wondered if maybe this wasn't just Randy's fault. If we hadn't made this Santar's story, or if it hadn't been a trilogy or ... "I think we fucked up," I said. "I think we really fucked up."

"Yeah," he said. "We did. I want to come with you to Robson Square. To finish this off."

"Okay," I said. "Then I want you to check out the stage at the Waterfront. You can sign that contract. I've got an appointment with Robson Square's manager tomorrow at two. I told the Waterfront we'd see them at four."

And I saw the same weight I'd been carrying for months unclamp itself from Randy's chest. "This could work."

"Yeah," I said.

"Yeah," he said. "Some flash pots, some fire, the guillotine. I can't believe you told Brad Bowen to sue you."

"Neither can I."

Randy nodded, then repeated our new mantra. "This could work."

"I could still use a few illusions for tomorrow," I said. "Something to keep the cast happy."

Randy grinned. "No problem."

And for the first time in what seemed like years, I believed him.

Robson Square, 2 p.m. I vaguely remembered that back when she did the deal, Jane warned us the woman who ran the Robson Square Theatre was a Gorgon. But the only Gorgon I'd ever heard of was Medusa—the hideous creature with snakes for hair who was so ugly that any man who looked at her would turn to stone. Jane couldn't have meant that kind of Gorgon.

"What do you mean cancel." It wasn't a question; it sounded more like a threat. I couldn't get a word out before she was shouting again. "You can't cancel on me. Nobody cancels on me."

"You don't understand, I ..."

"No, you don't understand. Do you see this?" She pointed to a corkboard on her wall where a week was covered with recipe cards that read, *The Initiation*. "Do you see what it says here?"

"Yes, but ..."

"Do you see *this*?" She brought out a calendar copied onto a piece of standard legal-sized paper. Sure enough *The Initiation* was listed with a one-week run.

"YOU CAN'T CANCEL."

Maybe her face couldn't turn someone to stone, but it wouldn't have surprised me if her voice could.

"If you'll just listen ..."

"No, you listen. You're not cancelling this show and that's final."

It was final? How could it be final? I'd barely said anything yet. "I'll see you for your tech run-through." Randy had already shuffled back toward the door, out of the line of spittle.

There was no doubt in my mind that if I even opened my mouth again this woman was going to rip the tongue from my head and pin it to her corkboard. But we were so close to salvation, or at least avoiding humiliation. And I'd just taken on Brad Bowen. I was not going to surrender now. "No," I said.

The Gorgon looked like I'd poured a bucket of water on her and she'd started melting. "*No?*"

"The show's cancelled."

"I have a deal with Rainbow," she said.

"Great," I said. "Work it out with them." I started toward the door.

"You can *not* cancel the show," she shouted again. But she sounded a lot less sure of that now. Then she flashed a smile, the same kind of smile the Wicked Witch of the West used when she tried to charm Dorothy into handing over the ruby slippers. "Maybe I can help you," she suggested, sounding almost as maternal as Brad Bowen.

"I doubt it," I said.

And as I walked out the door I heard her say, "But dear, you've already paid the deposit."

Deposit? I looked at Randy. He winced.

"Fifteen hundred dollars," she said. "And you're not getting that back."

We both went pale. "Excuse me a moment," I said. Randy watched as I left him alone with the Gorgon, walked outside into the hallway and punched a poster on the Robson Square bulletin board. Our poster. I hit it so hard that I not only ripped the poster, I made a dent in the fake wood panelling. I made a bigger dent in my fist. But I didn't feel the pain or notice the blood on my knuckles until later. Randy had slipped out of the office and was looking at me like I'd lost my mind along with my temper.

"She can't do this," said Randy. "Your hand ..."

She certainly seemed to be doing it. I didn't want to hit the bulletin board, I wanted to hit the Gorgon. Actually, I wanted to chop her head off, because as far as I knew that was the only way to kill Medusa besides getting her to look at her face in the mirror.

"Did you write her a cheque?" I asked.

"I wrote Jane a cheque."

"Do you know what it was for?"

"It was for Jane," he said.

This made sense. I would have written a cheque to Jane, too. But this wasn't over ... if the Gorgon wanted to negotiate, I'd negotiate. We were not doing this show.

I walked back in. Her smile now looked exactly like a Gorgon's. So, I hoped, did mine. "I've been thinking ... now that Rainbow isn't involved we can talk about the rent. The Waterfront is only fifteen hundred a week."

"The Waterfront. You talked to ..." She stopped herself. "I'll match it."

I didn't want her to match it. I wanted to leave. I had to leave. And I had to get that deposit back.

"And the Waterfront doesn't take a percentage of the door."

It seemed I'd somehow developed the magical ability to make people's eyes shoot death rays. We had another contender for the role of Satan.

"We'll forget the percentage," she said. Her teeth locked together so tightly as she spoke those words, I'm sure she must have chipped a few.

"And we're done at fifteen hundred."

Yes, she was definitely shooting death rays. "Fine," she muttered.

This was terrible. She'd matched the Waterfront's rent. She'd tossed the percentage of the door. I had to find something else, some other reason to cancel. "We can't afford to pay a technician union-scale to come in and watch two days of rehearsal."

"You're right," she said. "I'm sure we can find someone who will just let you in."

"What?"

"I'll cancel the tech call. Use your own people." This was killing her. And it was killing me, too. I didn't want to negotiate. I wanted to run.

Now Randy chipped in. "There's no way we can open Monday. We're just not ready for Monday."

Way to go, Randy!

"The show must go on," she said. "You can't just cancel an opening night."

"We've had ... technical problems," I said.

The Gorgon bared her fangs. Or maybe she smiled. It was hard to tell. For a moment I think I saw her true sea-green skin tones. "When can you be ready?" she asked.

It had never occurred to me to come up with an answer for that one. I looked at Randy, Randy looked at me. We were both thinking the same thing. We had a plan. A new plan. A great plan. We were going to do this in a month. When it was ready. With magic that worked.

"What if we call Monday a preview instead of an opening?" she asked. "If anyone shows up we'll say, 'It's a preview.' And if you need to, we'll call Tuesday, 'a preview' too. And you'll open Wednesday." She didn't seem like a Gorgon now, she seemed genuinely concerned, like she was trying to help us.

I knew we weren't ready, that there was no way we could be ready, but then I started doing the math. I looked at Randy. "We need to talk."

"Take your time," she said.

Randy and I went back to the hallway. Randy couldn't believe it. "Maybe we're cursed. Maybe we shouldn't have done a play guest-starring Satan. You're not seriously thinking about this, are you?"

"Do you think she's giving back our deposit?" We both knew it was a rhetorical question. "And if she's dropping all the fees the rent is covered."

"And no tech costs," said Randy.

"And Rainbow's no longer taking 30 percent. And we won't have to pay for new PR material for a new opening."

"So if we stay here ... if people show up ..."

I could barely say it, could barely allow myself to imagine it. "We just might break even." Even in our wildest dreams we could no longer imagine making money, but breaking even ... I could keep my comic collection, I could buy my dad's car. And if we could delay opening a few days ... maybe ... no, the show wouldn't be okay. There was no way to salvage the show. But at least it would be over.

When we went back into her office, the Gorgon's eyes glowed like the Balrog's. "I told you nobody cancels on me."

"Thank you," I said.

"Don't thank me," she said. "But enjoy your little show because I promise you that it will be the last one you boys ever produce in this city." Then she said a line she'd probably heard in a movie a million years ago. "You'll never work in this town again."

I didn't want to work in this town again. Or now. I wanted to disappear.

30

Dying Werewolves

That's when Heidi saved my life. She called. To see how I was doing. I felt like the biggest asshole in the universe. Her mother was in the hospital, possibly dead, and I hadn't called her just because …

Her boyfriend was a soldier, which meant he had a gun.

My guilt vanished. "Heidi, how are you, how's your mom?"

"She's good. Really good. She even stopped smoking."

I told her I was glad. She told me her mom was back at work and everything was almost normal again. "I really appreciated you taking me to the hospital and staying with me and everything. If there's ever anything I can do for you …"

"You want to direct, right?"

"Yeah," she said wistfully. "Someday."

"How's today?"

There was a long pause on the other end of the line. "You okay?"

No. I wasn't. But if I explained why, I wasn't sure if she'd do what I needed her to. If she took over some of the directing, I could focus on publicity. And making sure we sold some tickets. And had some tricks to do. And a soundtrack. And …

"Really?"

"You know the show," I said. And she did. Sort of.

"I won't let you down. I promise."

I was thrilled.

The cast was not.

I'm sure I must have slept at some point during that week. Probably when I was driving. I knew exactly how many tickets we had to sell to repay Uncle Stanley and I knew how many tickets we had sold. The first time I checked our box office numbers Brad Bowen's 30-percent take wouldn't have covered a plate of nachos at Bud's—especially if we'd wanted the special nachos with shredded chicken.

But one advantage of the Rainbow posters was that as ugly as they were, Rainbow was selling our tickets through all Ticket Wicket outlets and that meant all Ticket Wicket outlets had to put our posters up. Because they looked, well, obscene, I discovered the people at Ticket Wicket liked to cover them up—or tear them down—so I decided to hit all the major outlets each day to peel off whichever posters they'd placed over ours. After a few days of this I went to the supervisor at the main outlet and warned him that if our posters were covered or torn down again I'd report him directly to Brad Bowen, "and you don't want Brad Bowen pissed off at you." The look on his face told me he'd had that experience once and wasn't willing to risk in again. After that I didn't have to worry about our posters at Ticket Wicket.

I drove around the city and stopped at every theatre, record store or restaurant where I thought someone might see our poster and think that, "a rock and roll fantasy about magic and the occult" might be worth five bucks. The drawing was so rude most of the people working at these places either laughed or scowled before telling me it wasn't going up in their establishment. But some people agreed to put the posters up. And some of them turned around to help a customer for the twenty seconds it took me to apply enough tape so it would take them at least ten minutes to get the poster down.

My mom knew the general manager at the Vancouver Playhouse

and had offered to introduce me to him when I started on our show. "He's nice," she said. "You'll like him." I hadn't been interested until I looked at the newspaper ad above ours and realized the Playhouse wasn't just doing a show, it was a show about werewolves. And people who paid twenty-five bucks to watch a play about werewolves might be willing to pay five bucks to see a show about sexy sorceresses.

The general manager asked how soon I'd like to meet him and when I said, "How's now?" he shocked me with the answer, "Sure."

I raced over the bridge to the Playhouse office—which wasn't any more impressive than the Canadian Kidz office—though he had a cleaner chair to offer. I told him my dilemma. I had a show opening in less than a week, I'd barely sold any tickets and we'd parted ways with our promoter, which meant I was now the promoter and I had no clue what that meant I was supposed to do.

He told me reviews would help. "Even a bad review will sell a few tickets because it lets people know you're happening. You know what they say, there's no such thing as bad publicity." Reviews. Ouch. I hadn't even thought about critics.

I asked if I could put up our poster in his theatre. He took a look at phallic Santar, managed to keep a straight face and said he couldn't. "Company policy." I'd seen the Playhouse lobby, which had dozens of posters of all kinds, so apparently company policy only applied to posters featuring sorcerers with swords extending from their crotch. Then I asked if I could stuff handbills in his program. I'd made up new handbills complete with a warning—"Not suitable for young children"—that I was sure would attract attention, since I figured it implied nudity. I'd even whited-out Santar's sword, so the image wasn't completely offensive, just ugly. "Not sure if it's worth it," he said. "Our attendance has been really bad."

He was running the most prestigious theatre company in the city. He had great posters, a PR budget and I knew his show had good reviews. I figured his idea of awful would still sell out a night at Robson

Square. Maybe two. "It's summer," he said. "And it's hot. Nobody goes to theatre in Vancouver when it's hot."

I asked how bad his version of bad was. He made me promise not to tell, but that was a long time ago. "Last night we had twelve people. Paid." The werewolf show was dying.

I couldn't believe it. "We've already sold more than twenty a night. And we've got eighty for opening." I wasn't boasting, I was in shock.

He smiled, sort of. "Maybe we should be putting our handbills in your programs."

That was the last year the Playhouse ever did a summer show.

I asked our contact at Ticket Wicket how sales were at the Arts Club, Vancouver's other big commercial theatre. "They're getting killed," she said.

"How bad?" I asked.

She told me. "On the bright side," she said, "next to the big theatres in town, it looks like you're a hit."

There's a great German word, *schadenfreude*, that means taking pleasure in the misfortune of others. Of course it's a German word; who else but the Germans would invent a term for that? I admit I thought it was cool that we were outselling the new Dez Fiddler play about troubled teens—which was across the hall in Robson Square's other theatre—but all the other attendance numbers just made me want to cry again. Every time my Ticket Wicket pal told me how bleak the attendance numbers for the big theatres were, the idea of getting out of debt seemed even more impossible.

I called every media outlet I could find to see if someone would write about us. I found a taker at Vancouver's alternative weekly, the *Georgia Straight*. The paper had started life as a radical hippie rag, but had recently gone mainstream, ditching columns on drug etiquette and how to deal with "the pigs" in favour of cover stories on upcoming Hollywood movies. The reporter, a husky, long-haired guy in his thirties with a hemp shirt and jeans who was never going to convince anyone the paper had left its druggie days behind, came over to the apartment to interview us. He sat on my bed, Randy grabbed the chair, and I sat on the floor with crossed legs.

"So whose idea was this?" he asked.

"His," I said, pointing to Randy.

After we talked for about half an hour, he asked to borrow a copy of the script. I said I didn't think I had a copy, but before I could stop him Randy passed the writer his. "No problem."

I even delivered invites to all the papers in the city with reviewers, but on Friday afternoon—four days before opening—none of the critics had committed to attending. Because we were hoping people would call our place to line up interviews, I went to the phone booth around the corner to call the newspapers to try to find someone who might review the show.

Most of the critics I spoke to politely blew me off, but the critic from the *Province* said the show sounded "interesting." He wanted to know who we were and how we'd managed to hook up with Rainbow. He said the mix of magic and theatre sounded different. I said it was. Then he apologized, said it was a busy week, but if we held over he'd be there.

I knew a review was the only way we could get the show into one of the daily newspapers, so I asked if there was any chance he could turn up on Tuesday night. If I'd had money I would have offered to bribe him.

"Are you really proud of it?" he asked.

I have no idea why he asked that. Maybe he asked it all the time. But I'm betting that if he did, he never got the answer I gave him: "No."

He was sure he hadn't heard me correctly. Or maybe he thought I'd misunderstood the question. He asked again.

I knew I was supposed to lie. But I couldn't. It was bad enough doing a show that was going to be a disaster without lying about it.

"No, it's great, or no it's not great?"

"It's gonna be pretty bad," I said.

Yeah, I'm betting he'd never heard that one before. He stammered a moment while he pulled together his question. "If you don't think it's going to be, uh, um, very good, why do you want a reviewer there?"

I told him what the lovely man at the Playhouse had told me, that even a bad review would let people know the show existed and sell at least some tickets. I told him we'd spent everything we'd had, and borrowed anything we could, to put on the show. "And if we don't sell any tickets, we're dead." But I didn't stop talking until I offered one last reason, a reason that surprised me when I said it as much as it did the stunned critic. "We just spent six months of our lives putting the show together and if no one comes to review it, there won't be any proof it ever happened."

After a pregnant silence long enough to birth triplets the critic replied that knowing what I'd told him, he couldn't review the show. "How can I give it a fair review if the writer-slash-director has just told me that it, uh, that it's uh ..."

I understood. I'd blown it.

"But I'll see if I can get someone else to cover it for you."

"Really?"

"Yeah," he said. "No promises, but I'll see what I can do."

"Thank you."

The story in the *Georgia Straight* was seriously cool, because somehow the writer got across exactly what we'd set out to do back before Randy got sidetracked into creating Muppet Satan. The headline read:

BASIC BLACK

The article continued:

Rock music took many strange sidelines in the sixties and early seventies, but one of the strangest and least adequately explored was its temporary, drug-induced fixation with black magic and the occult. For a very brief time, rock entered into the world of magic and ritual—two things that, on a much less explicit level, seem to be at the heart of many older musical forms—as we saw Led Zeppelin's Jimmy Page flirt with the shadow of Aleister Crowley in his Loch Ness mansion, Jim Morrison turn his stage appearances into invocations to the Lizard King, and Dr. John anoint himself with gris-a-gris dust and prophesy in a gumbo thick croak. Even the Stones composed paeans to Lucifer, and rumours of strange rites among the members of rock's elite murmured through the concert-going throngs.

Somehow that all faded out as rock and roll became the province of even darker arts; the arts of balancing the budget and maximizing profits. Now when you turn on your radio you're more likely to hear a song about a pocket calculator than you are to hear hymns to Thoth.

This, to two young Vancouverites, seems to be a sorry state of affairs. Randy Kagna, an illusionist and jongleur with an interest in the occult, and Mark Leiren-Young, a science fiction writer with a sideline in parapsychology, thought that magic, mystery, the black arts, and sophisticated stagecraft could once again be successfully combined with rock, and so they created *The Initiation*, a "rock and roll fantasy about magic and the occult" that their company Black Metal Fantasy and Rainbow Concert Productions will be staging at the Robson Square Cinema from Monday August 10th until Saturday the 15th.

The plot is a slightly twisted modification of the archetypal good-versus-evil story; just different enough to be interesting, and not complex enough that much of it can be revealed here. It's

217

a story about two aspiring sorceresses who are competing to win the position of consort and priestess to the semi-demonic Santar; the things that happen to the lucky girl who proves herself adequately evil; and Santar's attempt to cheat Lucifer of his due. Enough said.

But this plot is surrounded and perhaps even overshadowed by what Kagna and Leiren-Young promise will be one of the most lavish audio-visual spectacles ever mounted by a local theatrical troupe. Flash pots will pop, dry ice fog will creep over the stage, demons and succubi will miraculously appear and disappear, mime artists will construct cages out of thin air, Lucifer himself will consent to make a cameo appearance (anything for the spotlight ...) and Paranoia will provide the (taped) music.

It all sounds like it's going to be good clean fun—maybe too clean for such a darkly Gothic idea—but still dramatic enough to give your average concert-goer a few titillating shivers and shocks.

As I read the story, I pictured an audience materializing to fill the seats for the ridiculously low ticket price of five dollars. Then I tried not to picture them demanding their five dollars back.

31

Muppet from Hell

Who knew bear skulls looked so tiny without the bear attached to them? Bob was wrong about Satan. Satan wasn't anywhere near as scary as Miss Piggy. At least Miss Piggy had some killer karate moves. Nobody laughed. Nobody cried. Nobody moved. Except Randy. He presented Satan like a father showing off his first-born child. "Isn't it great?"

I'd heard *The Exorcist* was supposed to be cursed, and it seemed to be true. After she pretended to be possessed by the devil, the only work Linda Blair could get was in a roller skating movie. I'd also read that a lot of the people who worked on *The Omen* died of mysterious, unnatural causes. Maybe Dougie was right, maybe it wasn't a good idea to mess with Satan.

And Randy didn't just want to build Satan, he wanted to be Satan. That had always been the plan. He'd written the song. He'd memorized the lines. But after we tried the microphone in rehearsal, everyone listening realized that no matter how much reverb we added, the audience was going to recognize his voice and think there was some connection between our narrator and Satan. That meant we had to find another actor or ...

"Mark can do it," suggested Ivy. "It'll be like you're part of the show. Like you're onstage with us."

Kyle liked the idea that if Satan was played by the director there was still only one person in the room he'd have to listen to. "Besides Heidi," and he shot me a look that was clearly intended to make me feel guilty.

Since we'd announced we couldn't afford a technician, we were forced to figure out the Robson Square sound system ourselves. The Gorgon had offered to let someone come in for a four-hour call for our dress rehearsal, but that would have been another hundred bucks we didn't have and Randy swore he understood the lighting and sound boards. "Nooooo problemmm."

And there wasn't a problem.

Sure, the magic didn't exist. But we'd rehearsed so many times without it that we could fake our way through all the major illusions and the walls and floors did look pretty good. Heidi even had the cast getting along. As I ran my first rehearsal in days, they seemed to believe the show was going to work—or they were much better actors than I'd ever imagined. The costumes were amazing. Our two witchy babes looked like witchy babes. Kyle used some dark eye shadow to age up and look almost ominous. Heidi came over to me, told me she hadn't been able to get him to wear his helmet, apologized. I told her that for the next rehearsal it was time to cut the lines about the women never seeing his real face. She looked relieved. And our first run-through seemed like … theatre.

Santar summoned Gamatria toward him, put his arm on her shoulder, her face moved toward his and they kissed until we heard the magic words ….

"What the hell are you doing with my girlfriend?"

Kyle and Ivy pulled apart like they'd been caught by someone far nastier than Satan.

We all turned to discover the voice had come from a tough-looking guy who was standing in the doorframe like he was waiting for a musical cue to announce his entrance.

"Wayne," Ivy shouted cheerfully. That was the cue. But Wayne did not look cheerful. He strode from the doorway to the stage without ever taking his eyes off Kyle.

"What the hell was that?"

Suddenly Kyle looked less like young Brando than young Woody Allen. Wayne did not look like a guy you wanted walking toward you like that.

"We're just acting, it's part of the play," said Ivy.

"Not anymore it's not."

He wasn't as big as Shawn. Or Dougie. But there was something about the way he moved that convinced me he could take out both of them without working up a sweat. "Wayne used to be a Marine," announced Ivy. She didn't say if he was on leave, or served his time, or had gone AWOL after killing his commanding officer with his bare hands. Heidi suggested a five-minute smoke break—exactly what you wanted in the middle of a first dress tech.

Ivy hadn't mentioned anything about her beau being an ex-Marine with a jealous streak. I introduced myself to Wayne, then asked to borrow Ivy for a moment. Wayne seemed okay with that. I asked Ivy if she could talk to her guy. Tathania had earned the chance to be Santar's initiate, but he was moving the goal posts because, like every villain throughout history, he had a thing for the good girl. The kiss was where we paid this off. There wasn't a lot of traditional drama in the script—way too much mystic babble for the sake of covering up the time it took to do the magic tricks we didn't have—but this kiss revealed more about Santar's character and Gamatria's confusion than any other moment in the play. It was, naturally, observed by Tathania and sparked her determination to do anything to destroy her sister and gain Santar's blessing, or at least his bed.

Ivy said, "Sure." Then she went back to Wayne, explained all this, Wayne nodded like he understood and told her that if Kyle kissed her like that on opening night, he'd jump onstage and kill him. Wayne wasn't a big theatre buff.

After our dress tech was over, as I paced the hallway alone, wondering whether we could get away with faking a kiss or somehow having it happen offstage, Annie came up behind me. "Hey," she said.

Other than giving her directions or telling her when rehearsals were, we hadn't talked much one-on-one since the scene with Shawn. "I've got an idea." An idea was good. I could use an idea. She flashed a sweet smile that reminded me she really was only fifteen. "I could make out with Kyle. I'm sure Shawn would be okay with it. He likes that I'm acting."

Now I understood the real reason Shakespeare's plays were originally done with all male casts. It cut down on the number of duels to the death. Next time I did a show—if I ever did another show—I was going to ask all the actresses whether they were single, right after I made sure they were old enough to drive. I thanked Annie, then thanked Heidi again, and was on my way out the back door when Dougie spotted me. I could see him following, but I thought that maybe, if I walked quickly enough ...

He was in front of me, blocking my way to the stairs. "What's going on?"

What was I supposed to say?

"Why weren't you in rehearsals the last few days? We need you in rehearsals, man."

This was kind of sweet, he may have been trying to be sweet, but that didn't register. "I've got other stuff to deal with." In fact, I had to get to Surrey to grab our master tape so we could have it ready to rehearse with that night.

"You got a show to deal with," said Dougie.

"Exactly," I said. "So I have to do all sorts of stuff like try to get an audience here."

"You're supposed to be our director, man."

I tried to walk around Dougie and he blocked me again. "I'm busy. Heidi's looking after the show."

"I wanna know what's wrong," said Dougie.

No, he didn't. He really didn't. "Leave it alone," I said.

"C'mon man, why aren't you at rehearsal?"

I'm sure if I could have come up with a wonderfully clever answer, that would have completely disarmed Dougie. Maybe I could have crafted a lie about coping with a family crisis, or a mysterious fatal illness. I know if I'd thought for even a moment instead of panicking over my need to get to the recording studio in time to grab the tape, before I raced to Dr. Bob's garage to check on the set, before I went to the Arts Club Theatre where I planned to spend the night passing out our ugly handbills to people as they left the show, before I drove down several major streets to staple posters over the spaces where our posters had already been covered up or torn down, before I tried calling reviewers and deejays and TV anchors and wacky weathermen again in the hopes of some sort of coverage, before I camped out on the phone trying to convince any friends who were still talking to me that they should try to sell tickets to everyone they knew, before collapsing on my couch bed for two hours of sleep, I wouldn't have said what I did.

"Because I've been told the only way I'm allowed to cancel this show is if one of the stars of the show dies." Dougie's eyes widened. "And if this show is as bad as I think it is ... I'll have to kill one of you."

Dougie didn't hit me. He didn't say anything. He staggered off like I'd kicked him with steel-toed boots.

That's when I saw that Randy had been standing behind me and heard the whole exchange. "That oughta boost morale."

32

Raise a Little Hell

Dougie didn't quit. I wouldn't have blamed him if he had. I think maybe I was hoping he would, that everybody would. I'm not sure I was genuinely prepared to kill anyone to stop the show except, maybe, Norman, Brad Bowen, the Gorgon, any member of the band and possibly Randy—but it wouldn't have been smart to double dare me.

I didn't want to see the audience, but I could hear them from backstage and it sounded like the place was full. I should have been excited, we had over a hundred paying customers, but as I pictured our stage with the beautiful black floor with no working illusions on it, I wished I could light the whole audience on fire before the curtain went up.

I found the strength to force a smile and went into the dressing room to send my cast to their doom. The forced smile was replaced by shock when I saw everyone laughing and hugging like the Whos in Whoville after the Grinch stole the presents, tags, ribbons and bags. Heidi saw me first, turned to me and smiled. "They're gonna be great."

Heidi had performed real magic. She'd convinced them the show worked. After everyone took their places, I thanked her and she took my hand. "You did that," she said. Then she offered me a chaste peck on the cheek. "They'll be great."

And maybe they were. I didn't watch. I couldn't watch even if I'd wanted to. I was trapped in a backstage closet with the microphone so I could do my Satan voice without being so close to the speakers that I'd create a feedback loop. But I could hear that the show was going fairly well—nobody was booing or even laughing in the wrong place—until Santar summoned the Devil.

First there was a huge laugh when Muppet Satan appeared from our miraculous floors. I could hear Santar's lines and knew he was kneeling to his dark Lord, offering his obedience on my headset. Then it was time for me to speak: "Are you fool enough to think that the Prince of Deceit would not recognize the scent of rebellion in his midst? If you do not wish to spend eternity bathing in the searing magma of hell, you will explain the reason for the mystic barrier to me—NOW." I loved the word "magma."

The audience howled.

I assumed this was because of how absurd Satan looked. It wasn't.

I got the news right after my big scene was over. While I was trying to deliver my lines in the most ominous James-Earl-Jones-as-Darth-Vader voice my seventeen-year-old vocal chords could muster, what Kyle and the audience heard was pretty much the same noise adults make in Charlie Brown cartoons. In *Spinal Tap* there's a famous scene where Nigel Tufnel creates the greatest amp of all time. Instead of going up to ten, this one stops at eleven. Our sound technician—the one we hadn't rehearsed with—had dialled our reverb to thirteen. So when Kyle taunted Satan again, trying to determine the limits of his demonic powers Satan replied gravely, "Blapblapblap blap blapblapblapblap blapblap blap."

There was nothing Kyle could do. Nowhere he could run. "Dark Lord," he asked. "Do you enjoy haunting me with recollections of my single failure?"

I delivered Satan's big speech—about his plans for his future

225

consort, Gamatria. I delivered the speech with gusto and a nasty laugh. I was proud of the laugh. I'd worked hard on those long drives to nail a proper cartoon villain cackle. So when I heard the laughter in the crowd growing, I assumed it was because of how silly Satan looked, not because the audience had just heard the teeny bear skull reply, "Blapblapblapblap blapblapblap blap blap blapblap blapblap-blapblap ..." for forty-eight seconds straight.

Kyle turned away from the audience as scripted, yelled at Satan and I yelled back, "A bargain with Satan is not to be trifled with!" which the audience heard as, "Blap blapblap blap blapblap blap blap blap blap BLAPBLAP blaaaaaaap!"

Then Santar and I had an exchange that set up the next big illusion—"the sceptre of the solid flame." This was the most important part of the scene—the exposition that set up all the action in the second act.

"Blapblapblap blapblapblap blap blapblap blap," said Satan.

I went backstage during intermission and saw that everyone had that slightly shell-shocked look you'd expect on Vietnam vets worried about Charlie in the tree line. That's when Heidi told me what happened with Satan and I wondered if any show in history had closed during intermission. I faked a smile, told everyone they were great, snuck out to the lobby and paced for the duration of the second act.

Bob snuck into the tech booth and told me people in the audience had eventually stopped laughing and started muttering to each other about the mysterious Satan. They knew he was spouting gibberish but thought, just maybe, that was the point. After all, maybe mortals weren't supposed to understand the Devil. Maybe the Devil was speaking in tongues. Some people thought it was the highlight of the show because everyone believed Santar was truly humiliated. He certainly looked mortified.

There was another bit of good news. Wayne hadn't been able to make it to the show, which meant Kyle and Ivy could kiss, which meant the ending almost made sense.

After everyone took their curtain calls, I snuck out to a side door and watched the 123 paid and 36 comped victims file out. The audience had the same look as our cast—like they'd just survived some terrifying ordeal. I didn't want anyone to see me. I wanted to vanish. I should have stayed backstage.

David found me first. He told me he'd been sitting right behind the band and they talked through the entire show, mocking everyone and everything, except their "brilliant" music.

"They were sitting right next to this guy with a notebook. I think it was the reviewer," David said. "If there weren't four of them ..." If there weren't four of them my little brother would have killed them—and possibly in the punching-Houdini-or-Randy-in-the-spleen kind of way. As it was, he told me it took all his self-control not to go after them when he saw them heading for the door. "We should get 'em in the parking lot."

"It's okay," I said.

"You sure?" he asked. He was definitely ready to go.

But as much as I appreciated the idea of beating up the band, I was pretty sure it wasn't the right way to end the night. I nodded. "I'm gonna go home with Mom and Dad then," he said.

I stopped breathing for a moment. "They were here?"

"They already went to get the car."

I didn't ask, but I didn't have to.

"It wasn't that bad," he said. "Except ... wasn't Satan supposed to talk? That was really weird."

"I know," I said.

"It was kinda cool though," he said.

"Thanks," I said.

He started toward the stairs. Then I saw ...

Jane. No. Jane was there. She'd shown up. I couldn't face her. Not yet. She'd want to know what had happened with Brad and what happened to our show and how everything could have gone so terribly wrong. It was time to slip back through the side door, go see my cast and hide and ...

That's where I was going when Tabitha spotted me. There was no way to pretend she wasn't there, that I hadn't noticed her.

"Congratulations," she said.

And the word cut much deeper than the sword Ivy had thrust under Dougie's armpit. I'd used the phrase "dripping venom" in the script to describe the way Tchara was supposed to deliver one of her lines to Santar. I wasn't sure what dripping venom sounded like until Tabitha congratulated me.

"Thanks for coming," I lied.

"I wouldn't have missed it for all of Medemptia," she said. "This is Ross. Ross, this is Mark." I'm not sure if Ross was her professor friend or not, but he was easily twice my age and looked it—even if he was wearing jeans, a disco shirt and one of those dorky thin ties the guys in Paranoia loved so much.

"It's Mark's show," she said. "He wrote and directed it."

Ross nodded and before he could say anything that might make me want to kill myself even faster, Randy bounded over. He was oblivious to Ross and stared straight at Tabitha. "Hey, Tabitha, you should come back to the cast party."

My eyes screamed "No." I didn't want her at the cast party. She couldn't. I didn't even want to go. I looked at Randy, pleading for him to say he was just kidding, or lie about the address. But he winked at me. He'd decided that if Tabitha went to the party, she and I might get a chance to finish what we'd started.

"Great," she said. "We'd love to, right, Ross?"

I wouldn't have thought it was possible, but Ross looked less excited about the idea than I did. But she was clearly going to drag him there.

The Bard was right, hell hath no fury like it. Nor did Medemptia.

33

Four Minutes and Nine Seconds

The party was at Ivy's place.

While everyone else sat in the living room and drank, smoked or toked, I sat cross-legged on the kitchen counter and watched through the doorway. Everyone looked happy, like life might go on tomorrow. But I knew it wouldn't.

It couldn't.

Randy was on the couch lighting a joint.

Heidi was snuggling her soldier.

Ivy was making out with her Marine.

Lisa had brought a guy who looked a bit like I did in the gorilla costume.

Tabitha was all over Ross.

Dougie was acting very non-Christian with a girl from the audience who liked the way he looked with his shirt off.

Kyle and his girlfriend, Wendy, and a bunch of other significant others whom I hadn't met yet were on the patio, listening to Pink Floyd on Randy's ghetto blaster and sharing a box of BC wine.

Annie was holding two beer bottles and offering one to me. With her perfect smile, impossibly tight jeans and tight low-cut T-shirt, it was like living in a beer commercial. "You want a drink?"

"No, that's okay," I said. If I glanced down I'd see her cleavage. Shawn would stuff the bottle up my nose. He'd somehow reached a détente with Randy. If Randy didn't so much as look in Annie's direction, ever, Shawn wouldn't kill him.

I forced myself to look in her eyes.

"Your show opened tonight. That's pretty cool. You should be celebrating." She was still holding the bottle for me. I looked at the beer. Okay, I looked in the general direction of the beer.

"Yeah," I said. "I guess I should."

I took the beer, took a sip and—"Is there any Coke?"

I hopped down from the counter to grab a pop and Annie practically caught me. She pulled me toward her, hugged me tightly. "Thanks for letting me do this," she breathed into my ear. "It's a great show. You should be really proud of yourself."

I'd forgotten about Crazy Shawn. I'd forgotten Annie was fifteen. At least my body had until a large hand grabbed my wrist. All lustful thoughts evaporated and were instantly replaced with knowledge of certain death.

"Hey." It was Shawn. I was dead.

Annie looked at me, looked at Shawn. The music stopped playing, the fridge stopped humming, Shawn pulled me toward him, I braced myself and ...

He hugged me.

"Nice show tonight man. Wasn't my girl great?"

"Awesome," I said.

"Thanks man," said Shawn. "I'm so proud of her."

As Shawn let me go, Annie appeared behind me and kissed me on the cheek. Then she kissed Shawn. When it looked like the two of them might start taking their clothes off in the kitchen, I decided to visit the living room.

I settled on the couch next to Randy. We'd just acknowledged each other when Jane sat on the other side of him. She wanted to congratulate us. Randy wanted to score. With a wave of his hand, he made a rose appear for her.

"Sorry Randy," she said. "I already have a guy."

"Yeah, right," he said. "Who?"

"Me," I said. I don't know why I said it, probably because I was tired of watching them flirt.

Jane started to laugh, then stopped herself. She saw the moment to tease Randy back. "It's true," she said.

"You know you want me," Randy said.

"No," she said. "I've been after Mark since the moment I saw him."

Okay, I could play, too. "It's true, Randy, we've been having a wild affair. Do you really think she took off to Calgary? Alone? Do you really think I've been spending every night with our band?"

Randy started to laugh and the laugh stung. The idea that Jane could want me cracked him up. It cracked Jane up, too. Everyone was watching and I felt even geekier than I had when I learned about Muppet Satan's inaudible debut.

That's when Jane leaned across Randy, toward me. "C'mere, baby."

I moved toward her just as the song *Emotional Rescue* started playing on Randy's boom box and that's when Jane started to kiss me. It was obviously a joke, a way to shut Randy up and see how embarrassed I'd get, how fast I'd pull away. But I didn't flinch, I acted like this was exactly what I was expecting, like we'd been making out for months.

I'd been scared by a lot of things that summer and now, a few hours after I'd watched all my dreams evaporate in a half-empty theatre, the most beautiful woman in a room full of beautiful women was kissing me.

I know exactly how long my tongue was in her mouth—*Emotional Rescue* is four minutes and nine seconds—and when it ended, it was Jane who came up for air. I smiled like Jane and I made out like this every night. "At last our love is finally out in the open."

"Uh, yeah," said Jane.

"Tongue," mumbled Randy. "There was tongue. I know you were kidding but ..."

Jane was still looking at me, trying to figure me out. I don't know what she'd expected. But that wasn't it. "I need another drink," she said.

"I'll get you one," I said.

It wasn't the triumph I'd dreamed of for our big premiere, but it would have to do.

34

Bad Publicity

By the time the taxi dropped us home I'd had eight bottles of beer and the most amazing kiss of my life. I knew I'd sleep well.

I took off all my clothes, tossed them on the floor and passed out. I was hoping I'd dream about the kiss, about Jane, but for the first time in weeks, I didn't dream at all. The good part was—no nightmares. The show had opened. We'd survived. And there were just four more days to go before we closed, cleared out of the theatre and I got my life back and had to decide what to do with it now that I wasn't going to be rich and famous.

I was out cold when I heard the door slam. I'd assumed whoever Randy had worked his magic on had left so I pulled a pillow over my head to shut out the noise of Randy making his morning coffee.

"Wake up," he said.

I grunted. I didn't want to wake up. Maybe he wasn't talking to me. Maybe someone had passed out on our floor. "Mark, wake up."

Damn. "What?" I opened my eyes and started fumbling for my glasses. I missed and knocked over a beer bottle. I heard it roll off the table and watched it bounce onto the floor. As it landed on what I suspect had once been pizza I looked up at Randy. He was pacing and when I first saw him his back was to me. Then he turned. Even without my glasses, I could see that Randy looked like he'd been shot.

"We got reviewed."

"It's bad, right? Can I go back to sleep now?"

"Read it."

"I don't have my glasses." I squinted and saw the room, which looked like a bachelor pad by Monet. The whole place was covered with pizza boxes, abandoned beer bottles and empty pop tins. It smelled like stale smoke, stale beer, stale pizza, stale McDonald's fries and stale incense.

My bed still smelled like almond oil. I hadn't changed the sheets since I'd moved in. I didn't know you were supposed to change sheets. And even if I had, I still wouldn't have done it. I liked that I'd shared my bed with someone who'd covered me with almond oil, someone I'd covered with almond oil.

I tried to pull a pillow over my head, but Randy's voice stopped me: "Rock fantasy turns into farce." Even without my glasses, even without looking at him, I knew he was reading the damn headline. Randy was holding the paper like it was diseased, so I knew it was less of a review than an obituary. He hardly had to look at it to start reciting the words. He'd already memorized the first few paragraphs.

"A comedy opened last night at Robson Square. The trouble is, it was supposed to be a serious play or, as the posters put it, 'a rock and roll fantasy about magic and the occult.'"

Randy kept reading. It didn't get better.

'Rock fantasy' turns into farce

The production, entitled *The Initiation*, gets off to a giggling start when a narrator appears in front of a shaky set painted to look like a stone wall and intones, "Greetings, mortals, I am here to welcome you."

He then tries to lure the audience into the fantasy by outlining a nonsensical plot involving characters with Marvel comic names like Gamatria, Tathania, Santar and Tchara.

"The evil Santar is indeed great," he says.

Enter two pouty teenage girls with plenty of cleavage, one in a tattered gold lame dress, the other in a red and black outfit that looks like it has been through a Cuisinart. They are Gamatria (Annie Ferguson) and Tathania (Ivy Dewar), potential high priestesses of this evil Santar.

Enter, via tape and amplification, the rock 'n' roll. It has been composed especially for this thing by the group Paranoia, which last year supplied the music for the play *Angst*. It is imitation Pink Floyd, but a good imitation.

Centre stage is a wobbly wooden cabinet. The priestesses enter and exit on whim. The evil Santar (Kyle Norris) comes out of the cabinet: "I have returned. Tell me what has transpired since last time I saw you."

Santar has long black robes and a hairdo straight out of *Grease*. Two hooded monks appear and try to remove the cabinet. They run into 'the altar' which looks like a large cardboard container from McDonald's; it almost topples. A priestess stifles her giggles.

It goes on and on.

... so did the review.

Randy kept reading.

As the priestesses battle to become Santar's mistress, the music battles with the dialogue.

Santar tries to deliver a soliloquy. The girls return, one in a sheet. One of them is put in a silver pyramid that looks more like a pup tent. She magically exchanges places with the one who is not in this contraption. So much for the magic.

The second and final act opens. "A battle has been waged," says the narrator.

Santar calls on Satan who has a cow's skull with flashing red lightbulbs for eyes and smoke coming out of his nostrils. So much for the occult.

The story line is lost. Santar has trouble remembering the names of his apprentices. He gets them mixed up. One of them tries to murder the other.

Gamatria goes into the audience and finds a victim (Dougie McFadyen) who is hauled up on stage and ludicrously tortured.

"Why?!" screams the victim. "What did I do? This is wrong! This is stupid!"

"It was necessary," says Gamatria.

"What are you going to do for an encore?" asks the victim. "Kill me?"

"Yes!" cries Gamatria, who thereupon pulls a large sword out of the altar and, after much dancing around, sticks it to him.

This is the climax? This is theatre?

No, this is just a high school production that somehow wandered downtown.

I'd say it's worth seeing for a laugh, but that would be cruel. Better luck next year kids.

After Randy finished, he stood there, silent. I knew this look from the St. John's Ambulance class I'd taken. He was in shock. "What do you think?"

"It's not very well written."

This was not the answer Randy was expecting. But this was pretty much the review I'd been bracing for. And it wasn't anywhere near as nasty as the ones I'd written in my head where I'd savaged the writing, the set, the acting and our sanity. I knew the review would be bad, I just thought ... Who was the guy who wrote it? Billy Barton? I'd never read his byline before.

"What!?"

"I mean, the lead is kind of a cliché and—hey." Suddenly I felt angry. I was angry. "He didn't mention my name, did he? I wrote and directed the thing and he didn't even mention my name!"

Randy didn't share my outrage. "Congratulations."

"I don't think he mentioned your name either."

Randy looked more miserable than upset. But I couldn't believe it. "I wrote, directed and produced. You performed, produced and designed all the magic. And he didn't even mention our names. What an asshole."

"It's the worst review I've ever seen. You really want to be in it?"

Randy thought I was being a smartass. I wasn't. "Of course the review stinks. The show stinks. But we just spent six months of our lives on this thing. I'm not gonna be able to buy a car till I'm forty. And there's not even any evidence that we did it."

"So what do we do?"

"I dunno what you do. I'm going back to sleep."

When I woke up I learned Murphy's Law of reviews. I didn't learn the first part—that when you get a great review nobody sees it unless you show it to them. But I learned the second—when you get a bad review, everybody you've ever met read it and can quote all the nastiest lines. And they all want to check in to see if you're "okay." After the fifth phone call from an old friend who hadn't spoken to me in months, and who hadn't bothered to buy tickets yet, I unplugged the phone and the answering machine and decided to take a shower.

Our shower had strong water pressure and it was loud—loud

enough that I could barely hear the ringing. I'd unplugged the phone, but I hadn't unplugged ... the doorbell. I ignored it. It buzzed again. Then I heard a loud knock. It had to be Randy. He'd locked himself out. He must have been so upset that when he took off for work, he'd left his keys on the table. I turned off the water, grabbed my glasses off the sink, and snagged my robe. "Hang on, Randy, I'm coming."

I'd barely bothered to wrap the robe shut when I swung the door open, ready to abuse Randy and discovered ...

Sarah Saperstein.

But Sarah was in California. She wasn't in Vancouver. She wasn't standing in my doorway in jeans and a white T-shirt with a caramel tan making her blonde hair look even blonder, while I was standing with my jaw halfway down to my navel—which wasn't even covered because I had barely shut the robe.

"Can I come in?"

"Sure," I said, convinced someone had spiked my Coke at the cast party.

"You thought I was Randy?"

"I thought he'd locked himself out."

I retreated into the living room and pulled on jeans and a Green Lantern T-shirt. When I poked my head out, Sarah was exploring Randy's bedroom. The door was open and his waterbed and floor were covered with underwear, drug paraphernalia and *Hustler* magazines. The only tidy part of the room wasn't visible. The closet was filled with magic tricks—all of them carefully arranged and organized. "I've got to meet your roommate."

"Randy's a magician," I said.

"Uh huh," she said. "I know. You've lost a lot of weight. Have you been eating?"

That sounded like a trick question. All I managed most days was one meal at the McDonald's drive-through. When I'd started the summer, I was thin—maybe 180 pounds. Now I was 160 and officially qualified as gaunt. But that didn't matter. Nothing mattered except ... Sarah Saperstein was in my apartment. "What are you doing here?"

"Your mom told me you were here."

She'd called my mom?

That's when I noticed Sarah was holding the newspaper. "I just ..." She didn't want to say it. "Have you read it?"

"I think everyone's read it."

I sat on my bed. I hadn't had time to fold it back into a couch.

She looked away from me, down at the floor—at the newspapers and pizza boxes and candy wrappers and abandoned rolling papers. "I was at the show."

I was mortified. She'd seen it? But I was thrilled, too. She'd seen it!

"It wasn't that bad." She somehow said that like she meant it.

"Yes it was," I said.

She sat beside me on the bed. "Yeah, it was. What was the deal with the Devil Muppet?"

We both laughed and I tried to explain. But after I'd finished telling her how it all started after Randy decided to write a song, I apologized for not spotting her, not inviting her to the party.

"It's okay," she said. "Didn't really know what to say after so I figured ..."

"Yeah."

"Sorry."

"Sorry," should have been my line. I wanted to apologize for taking her five dollars. "Robyn liked it," she said. She'd brought her little sister. Of course, she'd brought her little sister. I didn't mind though—at least somebody had liked the show. "She thought it was really funny." She winced, worried about my response.

"Did she write the review?"

We both laughed again.

"You could've said it was *interesting*," I said. "That's what I say when I see a friend's show and it sucks."

Sarah nodded. "It was ..."

"Yeah?"

"Really, really interesting."

I felt better. Somehow having Sarah there, talking to me, joking with me, acting like I wasn't a complete loser made me feel like, well, maybe I wasn't a complete loser. Then it hit me. I'd been friends with Sarah forever, but she'd never dropped over just to say hi before. Something had to be wrong. I didn't want to ask and break the spell, but I had to.

"So, uh, why'd you come over?"

She shifted uncomfortably. I was right, something was wrong. "I was just ... you'll think it's stupid."

I couldn't believe that after witnessing *The Initiation* that she—or anyone else—would ever again be worried about what I might think.

When Sarah finally answered, she almost whispered the words, as if saying them too loudly might make them come true. "I was afraid you might ... I dunno ... kill yourself or something."

I started to laugh. I thought she'd laugh, too. She didn't. "No way."

"I thought maybe you could use a friend."

Neither of us talked for a moment. She was genuinely worried and I was stunned—both at the idea that she thought I might kill myself over a bad review and even more by the idea she cared enough to come over to stop me.

It was my turn to confess. "If I was gonna kill myself I would've done it before the show opened." I was joking, but it was the kind of joke that made Freud famous.

"I'm glad you didn't," said Sarah.

I stared into her eyes, beyond grateful.

And that's when she leaned across the bed and hugged me. The hug turned into a kiss. And the kiss pushed me back down on the bed. She fell over on top of me. It wasn't a long fall. Our clothes were off so quickly I didn't have time to put the coat hanger on the door, but I didn't have to.

Randy told me later that when he got home from work he heard us from the hallway and went to Denny's. When Randy finally decided it was safe to come in, Sarah was gone and he was holding the city's biggest newspaper, the *Sun*, reading a review that talked about how groundbreaking the show was, how there were some strange technical glitches (thank you, Satan), but with a bit of work this could be as big as Doug Henning's *Magic Show*.

The answering machine was blinking like a machine with a message. Okay, a lot of messages. There were dozens of calls about the new review—including a report from the Ticket Wicket box office saying we'd sold out the rest of the run.

But the call that rocked both our worlds was from Jane. She'd heard from Brad and he was wondering if maybe, just maybe, we could discuss the possibility of working together again for the tour.

That night the theatre was sold out. Not only did the audio work for Satan's voice, but when the show was over, the crowd gave us a standing ovation led by Brad Bowen, Dez Fiddler and the Gorgon.

We went to Bud's for the first time since the "incident." Belushi scowled, but he wasn't kicking Brad Bowen out of his bar and Brad was buying. "Jane was right about you kids," he said over our second round of Coronas. "You've really got something."

The tour would start in Toronto ... at the Royal Alex. The Alex was the theatre that launched Henning directly to Broadway.

By the end of the next night's show we had made enough money to pay Uncle Stanley back with interest. After a two-week holdover at the Waterfront we had enough money to finish the magic, upgrade the set and pay everyone.

I invited my family and all my friends—including Sarah—to the final night of the holdover, so they could see how the show was supposed to work when Satan spoke and the magic was magical.

Annie split up with Shawn and got permission from her mom to tour with us.

Ivy got permission from Wayne to kiss Kyle.

Lisa quit her job at Young Ms. to join us on the road as Tchara.

We had a new poster for the tour with a full-colour picture of Kyle—without a helmet—surrounded by all three of our female stars. They were firing balls of flame above his head. It was pure Bond.

My mother never mentioned law school again.

I was a playwright.

Randy was a magician.

Kyle and Annie and Ivy and Lisa were stars.

The Initiation toured the world ...

But it didn't.

Sarah had come over that morning, and she did wake me up, but as soon as she was convinced I wasn't going to kill myself, she left to see someone, probably her cool California boyfriend who hadn't just written and directed the worst show in the history of the known universe. And I went to Randy's room to borrow a copy of Hustler.

I really did kiss Jane though ... and it really did last the entire length of Emotional Rescue. *I'll always love that song. And I'll always love Mick Jagger for not being beaten down by the man into writing standard three-minute hits.*

35

Manifest Destiny

No one else took the review as well as I did. When I arrived at the theatre before the second show I told everyone the review didn't matter—but the cast was even more upset than Randy. After all, unlike Randy they'd all been named as incompetent. When the actors started to get into their costumes they shuffled around like we were producing a funeral. Even though Heidi had taken over, I was still the director. I had to say something inspirational.

"He said I can't act," said Annie.

"He said ..." Ivy couldn't even repeat what Billy Barton had written about her.

"I think I should wear the helmet," said Kyle.

I wanted to say Barton was an idiot, the show was brilliant and he was too damn stupid to see it. I would have sold my soul to Muppet Satan to make the show brilliant. But, if anything, I hated it more than Barton had. I knew what it was supposed to be, what it was and what it definitely wasn't. And if I said that, nobody was going onstage. I said something about reviews and how they don't mean anything. Annie still looked like she wanted to cry. So did Ivy. So did Kyle and Heidi and Lisa and Randy.

"He said I can't act," Annie said again.

"So prove him wrong," I said, trying to sound as do-it-for-the-Gipper-ish as possible. "Go out there and do a great show. Show everybody what an asshole this guy is." It was the best pep talk I could come up with.

That was when Dougie arrived, out of breath, and announced he'd just gotten off the phone with Billy Barton.

"You talked to him?" I couldn't believe this.

"I told him I was gonna kill him," Dougie announced proudly.

I was shocked.

The cast was thrilled.

I assumed Dougie meant the schoolyard kind of killed, but still—you're not supposed to threaten to kill reviewers. It's not professional. It was pretty funny though. All of the girls—including Heidi—hugged him.

After some discussion of whether Dougie and Kyle and Shawn and Wayne should track Barton to his home or wait outside his office, everyone got into costume and I retreated to the safety of my Satan microphone, while Heidi alerted the house manager she could let in the milling throng of thirty or so diehard fantasy fans who hadn't torn up their tickets after reading that morning's *Province*. Naturally, with no critic in the house and no band heckling next to the critic, Satan worked just fine that night.

I finally saw the show. But I waited until closing night to make sure I wouldn't be tempted to kill anybody. On closing night Randy fulfilled his destiny and performed as the voice of Satan. His voice was completely audible—I could hear every overwritten syllable. I wasn't sure if Wayne and Ivy had come to an agreement, or if Ivy just knew Wayne was skipping the show, but during our last performance she kissed Kyle—so the whole jealousy plot made sense.

Instead of concentrating on what wasn't working we'd focused on what was. The story, the acting and the music were ... okay. It was only the magic that sucked. Since this was supposed to be a magic show, that was kind of a problem. But once you got past that ... On closing night the actors had fun. And the audience seemed to enjoy the show. I'm sure most of the thirty-six people there knew someone in the cast, but their standing ovation still felt sincere. If we could have gone to Bud's after the show that night I would have been happy to buy the drinks—if I didn't owe every cent in my bank account to Uncle Stanley.

I never wanted to do theatre again.

I never wanted to see a theatre again.

University no longer seemed like such a bad idea. Neither did law school. Or hiding under my almond oil scented sheets for a year or two.

Show Biz Legends

As they say in the movies, or at least write in block letters on the bottom of the screen—*Two years later:*

Randy popped up from the pool in the new apartment complex he'd moved into. He was gulping for air. His face was red, he was coughing up water. "Are you out of your mind?"

"Thirty-two seconds."

"I held my breath for thirty-two seconds? I can't hold my breath for thirty-two seconds."

"Then you'd better get out of the handcuffs faster."

Randy looked at me like I was insane.

"Again," I said. And I slipped the cuffs back on him.

"You're gonna kill me," said Randy.

"If you're lucky." And I shoved Randy's head back under the water. To be honest, I think I wanted to drown him. But this time he was up and waving the cuffs in under twenty-five seconds.

He was thrilled. And exhausted.

"Let's get it under ten." As I snapped the handcuffs back on an elderly couple wandered into the pool area to use the hot tub. We both smiled at them and said, "Hi." They turned and left—probably to call the police. Randy bobbed under the water again. I had a hunch he wouldn't be inviting me to visit his swimming pool again anytime soon.

We should have given up. Randy should have sworn off magic. Kyle should have run off to join a travelling Shakespeare Festival. Annie, Ivy and Dougie should have enrolled in witness protection except, luckily for them, even though everyone on the planet, including citizens of Micronesia, had read the review, only 432 people saw the show. I should have abandoned plans to study creative writing and applied to chase the inevitable law degree. Instead, I decided that in addition to studying creative writing, I'd study theatre, too. I'd learn to direct. I'd learn to produce. I'd learn to put on a show that wasn't a disaster.

Once we handed over all the money we'd made at the box office, and everything from our savings accounts, Randy and I still owed Stanley almost six thousand dollars we didn't have. We paid him back whenever we could and between Randy's day job and my singing telegrams we'd closed out the debt, without interest.

Randy and I hadn't seen each other much lately. I was at the University of Victoria with Dr. Bob. Randy was still in Vancouver, performing, but not too often. Then his mom told him about a talent competition—the biggest one in the province—the PNE Performer's Showcase.

The PNE drew all the top touring acts—it was the first place I ever saw a rock concert, Bachman–Turner Overdrive. Trooper opened for them. My dad got me four tickets from work and gave them to me for my sixteenth birthday. I didn't know who BTO was, but I loved Trooper. *Raise a Little Hell, Two for the Show* and my fave—*Santa Maria*. For some reason I could relate to the lyrics of *Santa Maria* about being on a sardine boat with a whole crew of crazy people.

This was the same PNE where I'd thrown up on Sarah's runners.

Randy asked if I could help him put his showcase act together. "You can write and direct it. It only has to be five minutes long." But it had to be five perfect minutes.

I asked Randy if he had any new illusions, anything big.

"I'm building a sub trunk," he said. The sub trunk is what Houdini used for the original Metamorphosis. I knew we could build five killer minutes around a sub trunk. "Can you do it?" he asked.

"Noooo problemmm."

The Showcase was huge—or as close as you could get to huge without leaving Vancouver. The finalists played the Pacific Coliseum, the same 15,000-seat arena that was home to my Vancouver Canucks, the arena where I'd seen Trooper, Bruce Springsteen and Fleetwood Mac.

The judges were three Canadian "show biz legends" we'd never heard of.

My parents and friends thought I was crazy for working with Randy again. Bob and David warned me they weren't building—or stealing—anything this time.

But I'd studied directing now. And here was a chance to direct an act that could play a stadium. It was also a chance to prove to everybody, especially myself, that when I first hooked up with Randy, when I told everybody *The Initiation* could be huge and Randy could be the next Henning, I wasn't crazy.

I'd thought of *The Initiation* often over the last two years and realized we didn't have to do "real" magic. In a five-minute act we didn't have time for anyone to come onstage to test the locks or chains but ... I didn't just want to win, I wanted to put together five minutes Randy could do anywhere, anytime.

We couldn't use flash pots—no time to set them on a stage in a competition—so we'd use fire-shooters. We'd use handcuffs. And we'd start with the newspaper tear and restore because I thought it was Randy's most elegant trick—even when I wasn't pretending he was shredding Billy Barton's review. Then, when it looked like Randy was about to launch into another party trick, a beautiful sorceress would lead her two minions onstage, capture him, chain him, toss him in a sack and padlock him in the trunk in true *Black Metal Fantasy* style.

Even though Kyle was in theatre school and had sworn off magic, he agreed to minion with me. But this time he had to wear a mask. The rule in his program was that you couldn't perform anywhere else while studying, just in case another director somehow tainted your training.

Lisa hadn't acted since *The Initiation*—and she and Randy hadn't seen much of each other since she'd hooked up with a new guy who'd bought her a promise ring, but Randy charmed her into being our sorceress. "For old time's sake. It's just one show," he said. "Just five minutes."

I made Randy promise me two things. The first was that we'd rehearse for at least an hour every day until the auditions. That was easy.

The second was that he wouldn't so much as touch a joint until the competition was over. I'd realized that when Randy was stoned he giggled, like Barry. And we needed serious Randy, we needed someone who owned the stage. I'd thought this would be a deal-breaker. It wasn't. "I'll do it," he said. "But we'd better win."

The auditions were in a church auditorium and when we saw the place, all of us had the same flashback to the JCC. We watched the other amateur acts and they looked like, well, amateur acts. The judges barely acknowledged each performer. One older male judge was reading a book and didn't appear to be glancing up at the auditions.

Dr. Bob reluctantly offered to help with the sound, which was great except there was something wrong with the sound system. When we ran through our act at the audition, it was impossible to hear the cues we'd rehearsed with. We were all remembering Satan, but this time the tech glitches didn't matter. We'd rehearsed this so many times we could hear the music in our heads. Not only did the reading judge look up from his book, but the others applauded. We were in.

We moved back into the JCC daycare and for the next two weeks rehearsed and rehearsed and when everyone was exhausted and cranky and ready to call it quits or kill me, we'd rehearse some more.

We spent more time going over this five-minute routine than we had prepping all of the alleged illustions in *The Initiation*.

When the big day arrived we had to rent a van for the sub trunk and the rental place misplaced our van. Then we were caught in traffic. By the time we made it to the Coliseum, we were so late that I drove past the parking lot and the security guards and right into the arena.

The Showcase had already started. When I jumped out of the van and announced we'd made it, the stage manager told us she was about to pull us off the bill. We only had two acts before us—two five-minute acts. If we couldn't be onstage on time she was cancelling our performance. As she continued lecturing us on the importance of punctuality I tuned her out, transformed into a drill sergeant and ordered Randy and Lisa to get changed and Kyle to prep the fire-shooters. I laid out the chains, the newspapers and the cuffs. We moved in sync, like we'd always planned to go on with less than ten minutes to prep. Randy was breathing hard when he got backstage in costume—but we had two whole minutes to spare. We nodded at each other. Kyle and I pulled on our hoods. There were only a few seconds of darkness between the moment a twelve-year-old violin prodigy finished his song and Kyle and I had to set the trunk, with the chains on top of it—and cover it with a black cloth.

When the soundman hit *The Grand Illusion*, Kyle and I watched from one side of the wings and Lisa from the other as Randy strutted out and nailed the newspaper trick. As he savoured his applause, Lisa strode out and blasted a ball of fire that exploded right in front of Randy's face. The audience oohed. As Randy turned to look at Lisa, Kyle and I appeared from the other side and grabbed him. Randy tried to fight us off, but once we'd subdued him, Lisa snapped the handcuffs in place. Somehow the microphone even picked up the click of the cuffs.

Then Kyle and I wrapped Randy in chains, lifted him into the sack, tossed him in the crate and Lisa snapped the locks shut. We handed her the curtain, she lifted it. Once, twice and ...

Lisa was gone and Randy was holding the curtain. The audience went wild as Randy gestured for Kyle and me to unlock the box. When we lifted the bag out and removed it to reveal Lisa—in chains and cuffs—everyone in the stadium cheered.

Randy turned and acknowledged the audience with a nod, just like we'd practised a hundred times and ... black out.

We were off so quickly—complete with all our gear—the next act wasn't ready to go on.

Backstage at the Coliseum we knew we'd done everything exactly the way we'd rehearsed it, better than we'd rehearsed it, but as they called out the names of the runner-ups, our hopes slowly deflated until the emcee announced the Grand Prize winner ... "Randyyyyyyyy Kagna."

Kyle, Lisa and I shoved a shell-shocked Randy onstage—so he could run out and accept his trophy and an oversized cheque for $1,500. Then the emcee introduced Randy with the name I'd suggested for the show, "The Master of Fantasy," and the crowd went wild.

After he floated offstage we cheered, we screamed, we hugged each other and that night we had a party at Randy's new apartment. Randy got very stoned, I drank at least three ciders, and we both kept touching the trophy to make sure it was real, that we'd really won, that even if it was just for one night, we were huge.

The Initiation was finally over.

Acknowledgements and Escape Acts

It was going to be the greatest show ever. It was going to make us famous. It was going to change our lives. To paraphrase my man Meat Loaf, one out of three ain't bad.

With Johnny Carson long gone, I'm going to imagine I'm on my current favourite talk show and Stephen Colbert is interviewing me about this book, abusing me for the politics, or the lack of politics, or for being Canadian, or for the fact that I wrote that a bear's skull is not that scary.

And I suspect the first question he'd ask is, "what's true and what's truthy?"

Several people who were part of *The Initiation* checked the manuscript to make sure I was recalling things as accurately as possible and that any changes were intentional.

So ... While I've occasionally shifted the timeline, or taken liberties with details—sometimes on purpose, sometimes because hey, this was a long time ago and my memory tends to be more kaleidoscopic than photographic—Satan really did look that silly, the write-ups of the show are verbatim and every incident in here happened. Most of the names have been changed and there are a few people not mentioned who were part of the story, but were magically transformed into composites both to create plausible deniability for anyone who wants it and to make for a less confusing read.

Thanks to Judy Dodek for booking me for my first ever magic gig; Denise and Jim Hogg for loaning me their garage and their son; Sharon Lax for her words of support and warning; Stacey Becker, Wayne Hubbs, Lee (who made us vow never to use her real name), Pablo Policzer, Stanley Rule, Stanley Wosk and Pat Schandl for their magical assistance; the gang from Big One Fantasy (for allowing me to master the art of gorilla-grams); the gang from the Comicshop (who not only displayed the infamous poster, but sold tickets for us) and anyone whose names I've forgotten after all these years (or who I'm not ID'ing in order to avoid outing the people whose names were changed).

And a magical bouquet to the people who helped turn these memories into a memoir. Thanks to Wray Arenz, Laurie Channer, Jackson Davies, TJ Dawe, Terry Fallis, Will Ferguson, Terry Glavin, John Gray, Grant Lawrence, John Lekich, Andrea Moodie, Art Norris, Shannon Rupp, Joan Watterson, Tony Wosk, Steve Westren, David L. Young and Darron Leiren-Young for their suggestions; Warren Sheffer for his legal and logical advice and the always-amazing editor Barbara Pulling for helping me make sense of the stories that are here and advising me on what to leave out.

Mahalo nui loa to Ian Ferguson for all his encouragement and advice and Tav Rayne for her encouragement, questions, design concepts, for fighting me when I tried to cut the nose job and Bunny Foo Foo and for pushing me to send this to Harbour. Thanks to my parents Carol and Hall Leiren for their love and support. And a bonus tip for Colleen's in Haiku and the Topanga Cafe in Vancouver for keeping me fed while giving me time and space to write and edit. Thanks to Silas White, Anna Comfort O'Keeffe and the entire team at Harbour for making one of my earliest writing dreams come true. And thank you for reading this book, heck for reading any book in the age of the interweb. Since you've made it past the thank yous, here's one more quick coda. Nope, we're not eating shawarmas with Iron Man and the Incredible Hulk ...

Not long after Randy won the PNE Showcase, I landed a job as a student intern at the *Province* newspaper. Their kindly theatre critic had moved on—and we never did meet—but Billy Barton (still not his real name) was on staff. I'd been writing for the paper for almost three months when I heard someone call Billy's name in the newspaper's cafeteria. The mysterious Billy got into the elevator. I forgot about my lunch break and caught the next elevator to the editorial floor, where I hovered outside Billy's office. I could see there was someone behind the vertical blinds. I walked in and introduced myself.

"I know who you are," he said, surprising me. He sounded nervous. He looked nervous. "I'm sorry," he said. "I know the review was pretty bad."

"That's okay," I said. "The show was pretty bad."

His fear vanished. He admitted that from the moment he heard I'd been hired he'd started ducking me. "Right after I did the review, some guy phoned up and said he was going to kill me. He called a bunch of times, I thought ..."

He didn't finish, but it was clear what he thought: he'd thought it was me.

"No way!" I said, as if I couldn't imagine anyone crazy enough to make a call like that.

"So I was kind of worried you might, I don't know, attack me or something. That's the only review I ever wrote," he said, "so it was great to land such a ..." He stopped himself to avoid insulting me further. I got it. Savage critiques are always better reads than raves, and way more fun to write, so if you're only getting one play to review for your portfolio, you kind of pray for a stinker.

I didn't need to talk about the show anymore. I'd met him. I had a face to go with the byline. And I didn't need to be reminded of the disaster that was *The Initiation*. Then, just as I was leaving, he said there was one thing he did regret about the review. "The writing was actually pretty good," he said. "Classic comic book fantasy stuff. I'd wanted to say that in the review, but I only had six hundred words and you know how it is. If I'd put that in it would have ruined the flow."

I knew exactly how it was.

I flashed back to Sarah wondering if I was going to kill myself, to Randy wondering if he should kill himself, to Dougie, wondering if he should kill Billy Barton. I edged to the door as he stopped me with one more question. "You wrote *Angst* too, right?"

He thought I'd written *Angst*? He'd seen *The Initiation* and thought I was good enough to write *Angst*? I went back to my desk to decide whether I should kill him myself or call Dougie.

I did neither, but when I got a job not long afterwards as a theatre critic for the *Georgia Straight* I never forgot how many ripples a review can create.

A few years later I interviewed Doug Henning by phone for the *Georgia Straight* and ended the interview by asking if I could meet him after his show in Vancouver. And I asked if I could bring a friend. He said he'd enjoyed our interview and he'd love to meet.

I took Randy. After watching a magical magic show from the kind of prime seats critics always get, we met our hero at the stage door of the Playhouse Theatre. We got to talk to him just long enough to thank him for inspiring our dreams.

ALEX WATERHOUSE-HAYWARD

About the Author

Mark Leiren-Young is the author of the comic memoir *Never Shoot a Stampede Queen—A Rookie Reporter in the Cariboo* (Heritage), which won the 2009 Stephen Leacock Medal for Humour. A stage version of the book (adapted by Mark) debuted with Western Canada Theatre Company in Kamloops in 2013. Mark is adapting the book as a film for Middle Child Productions.

Born and raised in Vancouver, Mark has always been equally passionate about journalism and theatre and received a BFA in Theatre and Creative Writing from the University of Victoria.

As a journalist Mark has written for *TIME, Maclean's, The Hollywood Reporter* and most of Canada's daily newspapers. A regular contributor to *The Vancouver Sun, TheTyee.ca, The Georgia Straight* and *The Walrus*, Mark has interviewed hundreds of celebrities ranging from William Shatner to Salman Rushdie. He has written two non-comic books of non-fiction—*The Green Chain—Nothing is Ever Clear Cut* (Heritage), a collection of interviews dealing with the future of our forests and *This Crazy Time* (Knopf) written with/about controversial environmentalist Tzeporah Berman.

As a playwright Mark has written comedy, drama, plays for young audiences, musicals, revues and in 2012 he debuted his first piece as a solo performer—*Greener Than Thou*, an autobiographcal comic monologue about the challenges of going green. His plays have been produced throughout North America and also staged in Europe and Australia. *Shylock* and *Articles of Faith* are published by Anvil Press.

Mark has received three Writers Guild of Canada nominations for his work—two for his radio dramas and the third and most recent for the script for his award-winning debut feature film, *The Green Chain*, which he directed and produced. He wrote and co-starred in the EarthVision award-winning TV special *Greenpieces: The World's First Eco-Comedy*, featuring his comedy duo Local Anxiety.

Mark is a lifelong magic and comic fan and scripted the premiere episode of the documentary series about the history of magic, *Grand Illusions*. Two of his favourite projects were developing TV shows that never made it to the screen—a modern teen twist on *Tales From the Crypt* and an adaptation of Marvel's *Moon Knight*. He is still the proud owner of *The Brave and the Bold* issues 28, 29 and 30 (first appearances of the Justice League). He splits his time between Vancouver, BC and Haiku, Maui.